THE
GRAY CHOICE

SHAUN HAYES

THE GRAYCHOICE

LESSONS ON MY JOURNEY FROM BIG-TIME
BANKING TO THE BIG HOUSE (and back)

Paige Publishing Group

Paige Publishing Group
Attention: Permissions Coordinator
400 North Fifth Street
Suite 109
St. Charles, MO 63301
501.299.5527
PaigePublishingGroup.com

ISBN: 979-8-9871814-0-9 (paperback)
ISBN: 979-8-9871814-1-6 (ebook)

Ordering Information:
Special discounts are available on quantity purchases by corporations, associations, and others. For details, contact Jane Fordyce at 501.294.2800 or Jane@shaunhayes.com.

For my readers.

I have lived an unbelievably extraordinary life that I am sharing with you in this book. Success beyond my wildest dreams and failures so deep that they changed me at my core. I only hope you will experience the highs I have and that this book keeps you from experiencing my lows.

TABLE OF CONTENTS

INTRODUCTION

It can always be worse, my dad would say, though I didn't used to believe him.

How could it be worse?

Believe me. It can be worse in ways you can never imagine.

When someone spirals or gets in trouble, it's natural to judge them and look down on them from your high horse, wondering how they could have fallen so far.

I'm not sure I understood this until it happened to me. Shaun R. Hayes, former banker, multimillionaire, and convicted felon— BOP Register number 45783-044.

I have no reason to look down on anyone anymore. My journey has forever changed me.

Anybody who thinks they're somehow better, more principled, or more virtuous is lying to themself.

A lawyer once wrote a book estimating that the average professional commits three felonies a day, and I think that's probably accurate. It was for me, anyway, during the years I spent operating in the gray, using loopholes and moral ambiguities to achieve astronomical success.

It reminds me of the plane flights a buddy and I would take to visit one of our operations. My friend Rich, a pilot, would fly the plane and I would sit in the co-pilot seat next to him. During the first few trips when Rich asked me to fly the plane, I said no. But on a cold February day, he asked again, and under his guidance I begrudgingly took over the controls.

I focused on keeping the plane exactly in line with the instruments in front of me. But after about 20 minutes, Rich wanted to take over again.

"In another five minutes, we'll be in restricted airspace over a large military base," he told me. *Oops.* While I thought I was flying on a perfectly straight line, I was a little bit off track—and being a little bit off track over time took me far away from my intended path.

Such was the case with my moral compass. Throughout my decades in banking, I thought I was doing the right things and staying true to the line of black and white. But little by little, my ethical decisions took me in the wrong direction, and it ended up costing me my family, my friends, my fortune, and my freedom.

Nothing is what you think it is until you're on the other side. And then you get a whole different kind of education.

CHAPTER 1
GOOD CONSERVATIVE BANKING

On my first day in banking, I showed up late.

It was June 1, 1982, the Tuesday after Memorial Day. I was fresh out of college and itching to work at United Missouri Bank (UMB), a huge downtown bank in Kansas City. I was the first generation of participants in the bank's new training program.

I showed up at nine a.m. sharp to UMB's headquarters wearing a light gray three-button Brooks Brothers suit with a red repp tie and a pair of cordovan wingtips. UMB's headquarters were located at the corner of 10th Street and Grand Avenue—the R.A. Long Building and the city's oldest skyscraper. I'd visited the day earlier and saw the hours posted in the window. Little did I know that time was for *customers*. Employees were expected to be there earlier.

In less-than-ideal circumstances, I got to meet the head of HR eight seconds into my banking career.

1

"Mr. Hayes, what are you doing here at nine o'clock?" Mr. Anderson scowled.

"That's what the sign on the door says."

It wasn't like they sent you a letter and said, "Show up on the first of June at 7:50 a.m. and enter through the security door. Tell them you want to go to the ninth floor to the personnel department." At least, they didn't send that letter to me. I guess I was just expected to figure it out.

It was an inauspicious start to a journey that would take me to the highest of highs and lowest of lows. Yet, despite these ups and downs, there's a solid reason I chose to work in this profession—cold, hard cash. I wanted to be a millionaire. Back then that was a lot of money, especially for a kid from Thayer, Missouri, a town with a population under 2,000 in the Ozark Foothills. Thayer was 270 miles away from Kansas City and 220 miles away from St. Louis. And because St. Louis was a little bit closer and bit nearer to my beloved Cardinals baseball team, I always felt a strong connection to St. Louis.

In high school, I was successful in sports and was the student body vice president and president. In college, I was interfraternity council president. I wanted to lead. I wanted to win. That hunger and drive served me well—for a while, anyway.

Banking was a curious career. My parents didn't have much use for banks. As small business owners, they stored their cash in three safes. My dad had a safe in his office that had to be four feet tall and a good 30 inches deep. You couldn't move it. My mother had a safe in the bathroom closet next to the towels and then a small one in her bedroom closet. My dad always kept $2,000 to $3,000 in his pocket. My mom kept money in her shoes. The last thing they were going to do was let the IRS know what they really made.

To my parents, money was something to hold onto and stash away, not something to give to a bank. People used credit cards for everything, and my parents taught me at a young age not to charge things that were disposable, like groceries.

As my father would tell me, "It's all about cashflow, Shaun." Needless to say, my parents weren't pushing me into a career in banking.

A professor of mine at the University of Missouri, Dr. Walter Johnson, encouraged my career path. With his shaggy salt and pepper hair sloping over the sides of his head, he looked like a guy who stuck his tongue in a light socket.

"Shaun, you should interview with a bank," he told me. "What's going on is monumental."

At that time, a massive tectonic shift was happening in banking. By the 1980s, the small business owner had more access to credit, and there was a shift toward sales. The silk-stocking banking of the time period that was based on relationships and personal connections with other bankers came with a haughty attitude—*let's meet up after the ABA in San Francisco and go to wine country.* When we needed a car, we'd grab a Chevy Caprice from the carpool.

The customer-banker relationship was built on information and power. Your local banker knew everything about you. A person's dreams and wishes, goals, and opportunities were in their banker's hands, and the banker said yes or no based on personal preference.

A banker was a god. That sounded great to me.

Banks were a hub of activity, a hum of waiting lines and forms and tellers and meetings. Banking today is so much different. Who runs your local bank? I'm sure most people don't know and never even thought of it. Everything's a credit card, a debit card, a credit score, and an automation. Walking into a bank today—which isn't a regular thing for most people due to apps and ATM machines—feels like stepping inside a McDonald's or Chick-fil-A, with a menu of offerings and quick service.

I applied for a job at UMB, had one interview, and immediately got a second interview that involved the company's senior management.

"What's your best marketing tool?" I asked.

"Being good conservative bankers," they said. I understood what that meant: you can't lose money you don't lend. Conservative banking wound up being a smart, safe approach during the 1980s and early 1990s—a period of volatility that saw more than 1,600 commercial and savings banks fail.

My first position paid $18,000 per year—one of the highest salaries of anyone in my fraternity. The training program picked up when I was hired. It typically took 18 to 30 months to become an officer. The program felt a little bit like basic training in the military—if the military were a cushy office job. It was a standard yes sir, no sir, follow orders kind of job. Some trainees succeeded, while others fell behind. After it was all said and done, maybe you got lucky and were transferred somewhere and came back with a title.

A week or two into the program, I faced a moment of truth. A management training company from Chicago sat us down to take a test. The first question asked was an ethical one.

"Have you stolen anything from this company?"

No, I wrote. I read the question literally. Other than being late, I'd done nothing wrong. Confused, I raised my hand and the instructor from the training firm came over. "Your answer is incorrect," the instructor said. I had only been there a week. *I hadn't stolen anything, not even a pencil.* If I had known any better, I would have already loaded up a half a dozen legal pads and a box of pens!

"Everyone has to answer this question 'yes.' Because you have stolen from this company." I was flabbergasted.

"I don't understand," I said. When you're in business for yourself, like my parents were, you approach things differently. But as I look back, the answer was absolutely yes—we steal time, and data, and so many other things that don't feel like stealing but technically are. That question represented the first of many ethical challenges I would face during my banking career.

Even though I joined UMB without a lot of banking experience, I got up to speed quickly. As a management trainee of the bank's holding company—the first one hired by United Missouri Bancshares—I trained in the lead bank and at a unit bank (what would be called a branch today).

The role meant I was associated with the lead bank on the corporate side. I went to bank-wide loan meetings, and then afterward, the leadership group would have a different conversation about strategy and the bigger picture.

They would explain why they were or weren't buying banks and negotiating deals. I had exposure to two agendas—the Kansas City bank agenda and running the parent company. I sped through the program and became an officer in 16 months, which allowed me to eat in the corporate dining room. For $2.20, you could get soup, salad, an entrée, dessert, drink, and attend monthly officer's meetings to hear what was going on with the company.

The building alone was a good reason for people to visit. It dated to 1906 and was inlaid with walnut and mahogany. With millions of dollars in artwork by painter Thomas Hart Benton hanging on the walls, it felt like a museum.

Banking was also very patriarchal. Women would come in for loan applications and have to answer sexist and demeaning questions like "Can you drive a car?" Banking wasn't thought to attract the best and the brightest. Back then, as the saying went, all bankers needed to know was 3-6-3—pay 3% on deposits, charge 6% interest on loans, and see you at the golf course at 3 p.m. I found that employees were either sharp thinkers or they got the job through their parents' connections.

We were required to wear our suitcoats in the office no matter the temperature. In Kansas City during the summer inside an aging building, it got *hot*. My brother-in-law Larry Snedeker, a successful lawyer, lent me some of his dress clothes to help until I could afford my own.

It was the era of regional banks before chains gobbled everything up. Commerce. United Missouri. First National. Mark Twain. At 22, 23, and 24, I sat in rooms with people who were buying banks. They were 30 or 40 years older than me, and I listened to them doing business with EF Hutton, VF Corporation, and these large Kansas City companies that I'd read about as a kid.

Two of my mentors were Mr. Huwalt (who was the vice chairman of United Missouri Bancshares, a.k.a. the mothership) and Bill Bolt. Mr. Huwalt would take the time to ask me question after question—so many, in fact, that I'd often think something over and change my mind. Bill, meanwhile, was more direct. "Do you not get it, Hayes? The answer is seven." A number of the trainees ended up presidents of large organizations, and I happen to think that the training we endured is the reason why.

Being ingrained in every operation at UMB provided a strong foundation for my career. It taught me how business got done and turned out to be the education of a lifetime. In Kansas City, if you needed to do a $15 million loan to these companies, you might pick up the phone and call someone at National Bank in Detroit. Banking back then was based on traditions and relationships—especially in a big little town like Kansas City.

Everybody seemed to be the child of a banker or the founder of a company that the bank wanted to buy. In Kansas City, there was one name—Kemper—that was the biggest of all. The family has been a force in banking since the early 1900s, following the path of William Thorton Kemper, Sr. who guided Commerce Bank. One of his sons, James, led Commerce for decades, while another son, Rufus Crosby Kemper Sr., became president of City Center Bank, which later became UMB.

Rufus's son, R. Crosby Kemper Jr., carried forward the family legacy as president of UMB when I worked there. Mr. Kemper, as I called him, was larger than life. Though he stood 6'7" and was a bear of a man, he behaved like a perfect gentleman to me and acted as an important mentor.

If we were meeting someone for a business lunch, he would say, "Shaun, let's show them a little house." That meant we were going to feed someone well. If we saw someone in a restaurant who did business with us, Crosby would send them an appetizer or a bottle of wine. Mr. Kemper had lots of little Crosbyisms. Another one was "Let's take him out on the *pawtio*," instead of patio. With each interaction and conversation, he taught me how to win people over and to be the biggest person in the room.

You could not *not* like Crosby. But he wasn't living in the same reality I was. Mr. Kemper didn't walk around in borrowed suits. He was born into wealth. His grandfather started the company, and Crosby carried the pressure of not screwing it up. I didn't have those same concerns. I could operate freely without worrying about protecting a legacy or namesake. It was fascinating for this kid from Thayer to get a peek into Crosby's world.

While Mr. Kemper could be nurturing, he also had a temper. For him, quiet was nonexistent. If he got angry, anything within his grasp or under his shoes was in trouble. Once, he kicked through a floorboard of a Seville.

UMB owned a bank called City Bank located in a development called Crown Center, and the bank's teller area was shaped like a football. Instead of the typical teller lines, customers could line up in about eight directions. I worked as the junior management lieutenant at City Bank. In a meeting with Mr. Kemper, he asked if anything went wrong over the past week.

As the gofer, I was tasked with giving him the update.

"Mr. Kemper, we lost $18,000 at City Bank on Friday."

He was immediately livid, his face turning crimson. "How did we lose $18,000?"

"Well, Mr. Kemper, when a teller was in the football and needed cash, they needed $18,000 at teller window 14. So, the cash teller put it in a trash bag, and the cash was supposed to be mingled (added with the other cash). Instead, the cleaner took off with the $18,000 in a trash bag." It was strange having to explain that to the head of the bank.

He especially hated dealing with real estate loans. UMB did not make real estate loans on properties that were non-owner occupied—Kemper found them too risky. If it was a real estate loan, chances were he wouldn't approve it.

He issued a memo on December 7, 1981—the 40th anniversary of the Pearl Harbor attack—and famously railed against real estate loans.

Crosby personally approved all of the bank's real estate loans. You could lend a business $10 million by yourself, but if someone wanted $1,000 for a piece of real estate, you had to talk to Mr. Kemper. The same loan that was approved on Monday could get turned down on Friday just because.

A civic leader once told *The Kansas City Times* that Crosby "has a way with people, a cross between intimidation and invitation." Mr. Kemper had his hand in everything—fundraising, development, politics, and organizations like the Kansas City Symphony. He was vacationing in Chatham for the summer and called in one day to check in on things. "What's going on Kansas City?" he asked.

"You know the president of United Telephone? There was a large article with photos in *The Kansas City Times* this morning about how he helped the symphony." It was like a hush fell over the poolroom before Leroy Brown started fighting.

Crosby was irate. He had spent a lot of money and effort keeping the symphony afloat and had given every symphony employee $2,000 the previous fall. They all came in and cashed them because they needed the money. And now someone else was getting a piece of the glory.

"Read the story," he said.

I unfolded the paper and read the multi-page article over speakerphone. "Mr. Henson got involved with the symphony not because of his knowledge of classical music—which he admits is limited—but because of his fundraising and organizational abilities."

I had to pause in between Crosby's screaming. It took me an hour and 15 minutes to finish reading the article aloud. I was soaking wet in sweat. We had loans from all over the state of Missouri we needed to approve. And guess how many loans we approved that day?

Zero.

Another time, I got a call from Crosby's secretary. "Mr. Kemper wants to see you, Shaun, and you need to bring the shareholder list." I wasn't even in shareholder relations. I took this huge binder weighing about 20 pounds into Crosby's office.

"We've got a loan to Mr. Gibson. And I noticed they were in your 'problem asset' report that came through this week. We need to talk about that, Shaun."

"Yes sir, Mr. Kemper."

"Mr. Gibson has about 12,000 shares of our stock. You think

you can make that loan look any better, son?" We were willing to extend goodwill toward favored customers while still avoiding risks that could put the business in jeopardy.

Things don't work like this today, as everything is more scientific. It was a different culture and a different world then, and if someone had a million-dollar investment, we did what was needed to keep them on the good list.

UMB taught me how to do things the right way, by the book. In fact, I didn't have a chance *not* to do things the right way back then. If I had strayed from their path, I would have been finished in banking before I turned 25. They drilled their process and taught me how to diminish risk. They taught me how to be a good conservative banker. For a long time, those lessons proved to be a North Star for me.

After I became an officer, I started thinking more deeply about the path I wanted to take with my career. I could stay in Kansas City and work my way up, and in 15 or 20 years, I could become a senior executive. But I would never be CEO since I didn't have the right last name. If I went to St. Louis, on the other hand, I could start building and establishing my own name. I could become somebody much faster. And that's what I decided to do.

CHAPTER 2
ST. LOUIS

Two hundred and fifty miles separate St. Louis from Kansas City. But in some ways, that distance seems greater.

St. Louis feels like an East Coast city with its focus on baseball and beer. It's affectionately called the "Gateway to the West," but Kansas City, with its western influences, better embodies that label because it opens up to the plains.

After all that Crosby Kemper had done for me, I wanted to get his blessing before leaving Kansas City. I ended up talking to him at a meeting with the credit people, the company's president, the CFO, and controllers.

"I hear you're going to St. Louis! Thank God we're finally going to have a go-getter over there. And we're gonna make some money," he told me. He turned to the controller, whom I had worked with at a unit bank. "Jerry, how much money did Pete make in St. Louis last month?"

"Twenty-four, Crosby."

"Twenty-four thousand dollars, Shaun! You're going over after a record month. We're really going to make some money this year. You're going to do it."

Jerry put his head down. "No, Crosby. Twenty-four dollars."

"Twenty-four motherfucking dollars! Hell, why didn't we take somebody else to lunch and lose money for the 10th year in a row?"

UMB St. Louis consisted of branches in Kirkwood, Arnold, Jefferson County (which always had frustrating zoning issues), Central City, downtown St. Louis, and Ferguson—the latter of which was up the street from the site of protests and unrest that occurred in 2014 after the death of Michael Brown.

After my transfer in 1984, it quickly became clear to me that I wasn't in Kansas City anymore. The cities have different energies, and they represented different realities for UMB during the 1980s.

UMB in Kansas City was all about blue-blood, silk-stocking banking, with the fancy dining room and valuable artwork on the walls. Our downtown St. Louis branch was across the street from the Mayfair Hotel. Our new corporate dining room, as we jokingly called it, was an aging hotel frequented by hookers. It didn't resonate the same way for clients.

The St. Louis operation was run by Pete Genovese, a kind man who grew up in North St. Louis County and previously worked at Mark Twain Bank. While Crosby stood 6'7", Pete barely touched 5'7". They were like the comic strip characters Mutt and Jeff.

Before interstate banking picked up in the mid-1980s, you couldn't cross state lines. So, while there were United Missouri banks all over Kansas City, Missouri (and we even had three "foreign" branches—Warsaw, Milan, and Paris, Missouri), we weren't allowed to have a branch just across the border in Kansas City, Kansas.

UMB's locations stretched south of Kansas City to the town of Peculiar, Missouri, all the way to St. Joseph north of the city. In Kansas City, everybody knew UMB. But 250 miles east in St. Louis, *no one* knew UMB.

It was peculiar, indeed.

Banking was all about relationships. But in St. Louis, I didn't have Mr. Kemper opening doors with his aura or a brand name that people knew or trusted. You'd go on a sales call and someone would say, "Who's UMB? Never heard of ya."

One thing we did was to organize focus groups. Senior leaders went all over St. Louis at night and sat behind smoky glass mirrors. There would be a dozen people in these focus groups, and the facilitator would ask the group, "what do you think of..." and "have you heard of..." and "do you know anything about..." But it was always the same. Our brand was unknown.

Information wasn't as easy to obtain back then, as I couldn't log onto the internet and look up business leaders online. Sorkins Directory, a popular business tool, was only getting started. So, I had to hustle and get creative to drum up business.

We processed checks on the fifth floor every night. I received a copy of the fronts and backs of checks for $5,000 or more. I'd look to see which company made out the check. For example, if it was ABC Printing, I'd check the phone book, find the listing for ABC Printing, and dial the number. "Hello, I'm working on my master's degree," I'd say. "And I need the information of who makes your banking decisions so I can send them a survey for my thesis."

"That's Mr. Butler. He's one of the owners."

"Thank you. What is his secretary's name?"

"Mary."

Then that afternoon or the next morning, I would call back.

"Can I speak to Mary please?" Notice I didn't ask for Mr. Butler. I would get transferred and go into my pitch. "This is Shaun Hayes with United Missouri Bank of St. Louis, and Mr. Butler does business with Mr. Jackson of XYZ." Big checks are coming across her desk, and she knows this other business owner (who, by the way, I've never met in my life).

But she knows that I'm asking for Mr. Butler and that I'm with Mr. Jackson's bank. I didn't say banker, but I'm with United Missouri Bank. I would say, "Mary, Mr. Jackson asked if Mr. Butler could give me ten minutes in the next week or two to stop in and introduce myself and United Missouri to him." She's not going to say no because I'm somebody important—I must be to know Mr. Jackson— and she doesn't want to be the one asking too many questions. "How about next Thursday, three o'clock?" she asks. *Yes, that works great.*

A good salesman's goal is to get the next appointment. That little trick got me in lots of doors in St. Louis, all with no prior information. It allowed me to go to cocktail parties where I'd run into business leaders. "You're Mr. Jackson's banker!" Yet, I wouldn't know Mr. Jackson if he were standing next to me.

It was a slippery tactic, a gray area of sorts. Banking came with a lot of gray areas. My boss, Pete Genovese, happened to be introverted, and I served as his fair-haired liege. When it came to anything social, I was tasked with the job. I ended up going to events across the city and took trips to Washington, D.C. all the time. You name it, I was there. Benjamin F. Edwards III, the head of the securities firm A.G. Edwards, had a show for his unbelievable collection of Asian art. At 25 years old, I was in heaven.

E.S. Gatch took me under his wing, too. E.S. (Elias Speidel) sold paint before working for a small bank in Clayton that got bought out. Pete hired him right before I moved to St. Louis. E.S. had gone to school with every CEO and every rich family in the city. He didn't know much about banking and didn't really need to. He was pedigreed.

We sponsored a dinner, and I gave a keynote speech in front of several hundred people from St. Louis's biggest companies.

Within a year I became a vice president, and in short order, I got promoted again to senior VP in charge of corporate banking in late 1986. With all the promotions and hobnobbing and hustling,

I was establishing a network of contacts in St. Louis—many of them 20 years my senior—who trusted me with their business.

As it turns out, there was something else that helped me establish trust: a family.

I met Sandra in UMB's management program. She was a year older than I was and went to work for Boatman's. We married in 1984. It worked great being with someone who understood the industry. Sometimes she would entertain and I would be the spouse, and at other times we'd switch roles.

We set boundaries and respected them. I did not poach her clients and she did not poach mine. But as soon as she left banking in 1986 to work in children's apparel, her clients began reaching out to me.

Our first child, Stephen, was born a year later. Being a dad has meant everything to me—I've had so much fun. I vowed to be the dad who coaches all of their kids' teams and who was always there for his children, no matter what. I didn't want them to feel a disconnect like the one I had with my dad. I wanted to make my children proud. That doesn't always happen, of course, even if you have the best intentions in mind. But that was the type of father I aimed to be.

For me, family is a special thing. I also recognized over the years that it opens doors in the banking business. Having a family reflects stability and values. Your family becomes a lead generator—your children's school or your wife's hairdresser are all fair game. All of these threads connect to build your sphere of influence.

Amid my personal growth, I still struggled to build my influence within the company outside of UMB's Kansas City power core. You couldn't wind your watch at UMB without going through the chain of command. Bankers with other companies could make a two-million-dollar loan while sitting at their desk. But at UMB, everything went through Kansas City and might take two weeks. With my connections and Kansas City training, I knew what I needed to do to get deals done, even if everything was a struggle.

At times it was frustrating to constantly swim against the current. I grew impatient waiting for the current to change or for my chance to move upstream. When the president of UMB's St. Louis operations left, I eyed the position. Despite my interest, for a long time the position remained open.

Even if everything wasn't falling into place, I gained lots of relevant experience. Instead of listening to the bigwigs make bank deals like I had during my training days, I was starting to become a power player myself. We were the largest shareholders in Centerre Bank, which was the blue-blood St. Louis bank. However, Pete Genovese didn't want to go to the annual meeting, so I went instead. They'd say, "Are there any votes no?" I'd walk up and give it to them, and everyone would ask, "Who's that 6'3" guy who does that all the time?"

By February of 1988, UMB wanted to buy Centerre, and they wanted *me* to make the offer. Here I was all of 27 years old meeting with these titans of business—board members included beer company heir August Busch III and Chuck Knight, who ran Emerson Electric with an iron fist—to deliver this message. I went with two lieutenants. These other executives all had drivers and Cadillac limos while I drove a K-car.

I arrived on the 13ᵗʰ floor where Centerre's executive offices were located and handed them a letter. "We'll pay you twenty-eight dollars a share." We never paid full price for anything, so that was the offer.

"You can leave," they said. I noticed a phone in the seating area outside the door. I picked it up and called my assistant. "Jolene, it's Shaun." It was just a chance for me to eavesdrop. Soon enough, the executives figured out that the enemy was still in their midst. Their security showed up and escorted me out. Was what I did wrong? Probably, but I gained a lot of information.

A longtime Centerre executive named Clarence "Cedge" Barksdale and I have laughed about it ever since. "We should have thrown you out sooner," he told me. Getting the chance to make a multi-billion-dollar offer to buy another company isn't a typical experience for a 20-year-old. (Centerre ended up selling to Boatman's, but we put them in play to make a bunch of money.)

The Centerre situation is a reflection of this era—a time when many banks were struggling. More than 1,600 savings and commercial banks failed during the late 1980s and early 1990s due to a patchwork of issues that included deregulation, economic downturns, and unrestrained real estate lending.[1]

---

1   Summa, John. "From Booms to Bailouts: The Banking Crisis of the 1980s." Investopedia. Investopedia, October 6, 2021. https://www.investopedia.com/articles/financial-theory/banking-crisis-1980s.asp#:~:text=The%20financial%20crisis%20of%202007,global%20credit%20disasters%20in%20history.

Amid all of the uncertainty, UMB seemed like America's strongest bank. We were confident and cocky. So much so that we turned down many opportunities to expand into other states. Buying two banks across the river in Illinois in 1986 was a big deal for us, as we often considered these opportunities but never acted on them. Crosby was the kind of guy who looked at everything but never took risks. We did, however, buy struggling banks in Tightwad, Missouri, because Crosby liked the idea of having a bank with "tightwad" on the checks.

Things were steady for UMB. But in my opinion, sometimes it's worth taking a chance and trying something new. As the 1980s wore down, I itched for more. Something else. Something bigger. Something I could run myself. It was a blow to be passed over as president of UMB's St. Louis operations—and surprise, they brought over an executive from Kansas City. I also missed a raise, which I had gotten like clockwork every 180 days. Others with the same title as me had company cars, but I didn't.

These slights forced me to look inside, and in truth, I felt lost. Yes, I needed to provide for my family, but I also wanted much more than that. My goal was to be a *millionaire* one day. I wasn't going to achieve that milestone by plodding up the corporate ladder.

While at a crossroads during the summer of 1988, I decided to leave banking and try a different career. Sandra had made the switch, and it exposed me to the lifestyle of an entrepreneur. There were company cars, lunches, and dinners out on the company, and much more autonomy.

What would I do next? I began talking to my clients in plastics, transportation, and other industries. The problem was I didn't have enough capital to buy a business, and all of these businesspeople around me were telling me the same thing: *Why don't you start a bank or do a bank deal?*

That wasn't my interest, as I was loyal to Mr. Kemper. I didn't want to become a direct competitor, but if I slinked away into some other field, it would be no big thing. At the time, I was also filled with doubt.

As it turns out, I shouldn't have been.

Perception is reality, according to Thompson's corollary. The perception of me was that I was this tall guy who wears three-button suits, Hermes ties, and light blue dress shirts, and even if I didn't have decades of banking experience, I had presence and charisma. Other people believed in me and saw something I didn't.

I had dinner with a man named Mike Cole, who had helped me with a loan on a house I was renovating at the time and had experience as a bank CEO. He'd worked out of St. Louis for three years and he wanted back in. As we sat and talked for five hours, he outlined an opportunity to buy a bank in northeast Missouri. I saw a chance to begin making money on day one with a rural bank.

It was a different strategy than launching a startup, or a de novo bank, like lots of bankers were doing at the time. A de novo bank might lose money for a year or two and break even in the third year. By year five, there was the potential for a significant revenue stream.

But this bank was in the middle of nowhere in the town of Kahoka, 168 miles outside of St. Louis. I didn't know what to do. As I drove those 168 miles, I thought of my career, my family, and what it was that would make me happy. As my tires covered the distance, it all felt right to me. Maybe Kahoka reminded me a little bit of my childhood and the place where I'd grown up.

Yes, let's do this, I decided.

After we signed a contract, we played the waiting game for five months before we closed. I'd almost forgotten about this thing when Mike Cole called me one day.

"We're taking this bank over next week," he told me.

On the third Friday in May 1989, I went to work and did everything as I normally would for any other loan meeting, getting our deals approved. As soon as the meeting was over, I pulled Pete aside. "I need to talk to you."

We drove to our downtown St. Louis branch, got lunch, and went into to Pete's office to go over everything. They got me on the phone with Kansas City. One, they wanted to debrief me, and two, they wanted me to stay.

Pete was the good cop, as he always was. Mick Aslin, Crosby's colleague, played bad cop and went right after me. He said the things that my mentor Mr. Kemper wouldn't say himself. "I can't believe you'd do this! We've invested seven years in you." They promised that if I stayed, I'd be president in five years. As it turned out, nearly five years later, the position would go to Crosby

Kemper III. I'm a very loyal person, and that meeting bothered me. But sometimes things turn out for the best, and it was my time to go. My exit had already been in the works. There was no turning around.

It was my last day at UMB. My education was over, and next up was a rocket ride.

CHAPTER 3
168 MILES

I never intended to carry three-quarters of a million dollars in cash in the trunk of my Buick LeSabre.

But there I was, white-knuckle driving down Highway 61 for 168 miles. The car's overloaded back-end drug so low it might have been shooting sparks across the highway. There was so much that could go wrong. What if I got into an accident? What if someone carjacked me? *Well, officer, I happened to have $750,000 in uninsured cash in the car. Can you help me find it?* It was the scariest, stupidest car ride of my life—one borne from ego and pride. It served as a good reminder, as I took control of my first bank, that I didn't have a clue what I was doing.

At UMB I ran a sales force. I wasn't a credit guy or an operations guy, and I didn't know anything about IT. I knew these things happened, and I knew they were important, but I didn't have experience in any of these areas.

Luckily, Mike Cole knew more than I did. He was about nine years older than I was and had experience working at Boatman's and other banks. He helped guide the sale of our Kahoka bank and became its chairman, while I became president.

Instead of seeing my inexperience as a disadvantage, I leaned into it and aimed to surround myself with smarter, more experienced people who had already achieved success. I relied on my connections to help me make deeper inroads in the community and raise funds, which was the first obstacle we had to tackle.

Bringing in cash happened to be one of my strengths—especially given all of the hustling I had done during my years working in St. Louis when I was trying to get people to notice UMB's overlooked operations.

With no controlling corporate office in Kansas City anymore, it was all on me, and it felt good to bet on myself. I didn't spend a lot of time worrying about what could go wrong, and maybe my relative naivete allowed me to dream big without reservations.

My accountant connected me with a handful of people—one of which was an older Jewish man named Milton Fry who treated me unbelievably well. Milton was a sharp businessman and led his family's moving, storage, and logistics company, Fry-Wagner Systems. He also served on numerous company boards.

"Shaun, I'm gonna give you $50,000," he told me. Support from Milton and others made me start to believe in myself. If he believed in me, why couldn't I? Milton had some men over to his house one night, and two of them put in $25,000 apiece even though I'd never met them before. One of them was Harvey

Harris, a managing partner of a leading law firm who owned a percentage of St. Louis's historic Fox Theatre.

Milton Fry's blessing opened many doors for us. People wanted to invest simply because Milton had invested in me. Bringing in these investments was a game of connect the dots, and I didn't realize right away that I was playing the game.

I'd help someone, and they would turn around and say, "My friend Joe needs some help," and introduce both of us. That happened every day. I didn't stop to consider what was developing at the time. These people had their own cadres of clients and friends and professionals, and every person I met was helping to put this bank on the map.

Another major investor was Marvin Wool, a chemist and entrepreneur who gave me $200,000 and joined our bank board. On the other hand, Leon Felman was worth tens of millions of dollars, but extracting the first $50,000 from him was like getting five million out of Warren Buffett. He was an astute investor and had a good deal of credibility within the financial world.

Suddenly, my life turned into one big meeting. I had meetings during breakfast, lunch, and dinner. I met with people constantly in an attempt to drum up capital. My record was seven breakfasts in one morning. I'd have meetings at 6:00, 6:30, 7:00, and so on. I might not leave that table for four hours (and leave a big tip). Sometimes I met with people six or seven times who never invested. *Their loss.*

Small-town banking is like small-town politics. There were four banks in a town of 2,000 people. It was competitive as the devil, and we were the outsiders. None of us lived in the town. Mike and I hired people to handle day-to-day operations, but the Kahoka bank, located near the town square in a prime spot, looked right out of my hometown of Thayer in the 1960s.

It was an odd building. One time, we went out to lunch with some executives and showed them the bank afterward. Mike Cole took them on the tour of the "secret room." Down a stairway, past a kitchen area and community room, and through a hallway, we made a left and opened the door to reveal a Masonic temple. The Freemasons had a one dollar, 99-year lease to hold their meetings in the building's basement. The entryway featured swords and other items on the wall, and it opened to a giant room featuring chairs fit for a king.

And this was underneath the bank's main lobby!

Investors weren't buying into this little bank in Kahoka—even with the Masonic temple underneath—they were buying into the vision for what was to come. One day, our low-cost, profitable bank in the sticks would grow and compete in St. Louis.

They were buying into the idea of *Allegiant*. I initially wanted our name to be "Alliant." In those days when they listed bank rates, they would arrange the banks alphabetically, so there was an advantage to being at the front of the alphabet, and not, for example, UMB.

There was one problem. There was already an Alliant Bank in Huntsville, Alabama. I called up their president and asked for the right to use the name "Alliant" for Missouri, Illinois, and Iowa. "I want $125,000," he said.

I didn't tell him "fuck you," but that's what I was thinking. So instead, Mike and I came up with "Allegiant." We pledged to uphold *loyalty* and committed to a better way of banking. In all honesty, we weren't pledging anything—we just liked the name.

We picked a challenging time to take over a bank, especially one that had been struggling previously. Commerce (owned by a Kemper, naturally) was divesting. Banks were failing left and right. But the timing also saved us some money. When you buy a bank that's making $25,000 a month, like the Kahoka bank, you expect to pay a premium. But banks at the time were in such a slump the premium we paid was only $300,000—which was next to nothing. A decade later, I would expect to pay a three million premium for that sort of bank and not even flinch.

We met with a law firm to make sure everything with the sale was correct and proper. I didn't have any real money at the time, but they wanted a floor of $25,000, which seemed reasonable. So Mike and I chipped in $12,500 each (I had to make payments to pay it off). I wanted a ceiling of $75,000, but they ended up sending us a bill for $109,000 because they could.

We got the deal finalized, received federal approval, and closed in October of 1989. In the final months of the calendar year, we made about $60,000—something a new bank might not accomplish until its third year.

Even though we made quick progress, I didn't let up on the gas pedal. I convinced Mike that I needed a company car. The drive to and from my house was a long way, and since I was going to be meeting with customers, I needed to drive in style. A car dealership down the street from the bank had a ruby red Buick LeSabre. It was the first new car I ever had.

On my drives to and from work, the highway patrolmen became very familiar with my LeSabre. "Sir, turn on your cruise control and turn off your radar detector," they would tell me.

Phone technology helped make the drives more productive. For a while, with a brick-sized mobile phone, I could get phone reception about 60 miles outside of St. Louis, and as the cell phone technology improved during the 1990s, I got up to about 100 miles of phone reception. I would spend part of my drive thinking and the other part of my drive making phone calls.

Some of my trips were riskier than others. After we bought the Kahoka bank, we had $1.1 million in vault cash, and Federal Reserve funds at the time were 9%. Mike came up with an idea, and it wasn't a bad one. If we took some of that cash and lent it to the Fed, at that rate, we'd make somewhere around $5,000 a month in federal funds. But in order to do that, we needed to transport the cash to the Federal Reserve Bank of St. Louis.

I called Brinks. They wanted to charge us $250 to transport the money.

Screw you. We could do this ourselves. For free.

That's how I came to drive $750,000 in cash down the highway in a LeSabre with Mike Cole tailing me. We stopped at my house in Ladue, a nice suburb right off the highway, eight miles from the Fed.

I had never been so relieved to make it home. We unloaded the money, carrying handfuls of cash in paper sacks. We arranged it in the family room, adjacent to the TV set, chair, and sofa. We put blankets on top of the money and slept next to it.

While the neighborhood was safe, we were concerned about the large window in the room that opened to the backyard. If anyone happened to rob us that night, they could have made off with three-quarters of a million dollars. If the house had burned down, it would have been gone.

We got up at 4:30 a.m., loaded the cash back into the car, and went downtown, arriving at 5:30 a.m. to find a row of Brinks trucks lining Fourth Street, joined by one ruby red 1989 Buick LeSabre.

All of that over $250.

People viewed our bank as a risk-taker (imagine that!), although statistically, we came to have one of the lowest loss rates in our region. Most banks would get the customer to sign, and then a year and a half later when things weren't working out, they would try to figure out how to screw over the client and take everything they had before focusing on cutting their losses.

We were thinking on the way in, *how do we lose nothing?* The real money in banking wasn't in doing business with General Motors or huge electronics companies. You'd only get 10 basis points—which are equal to 1/100th of 1%—for backing up a commercial loan.

The money was in the small business owner who wanted to start a little company and hire four people. They needed a hundred grand and pledged their house and paid the prime rate plus 3%. All of a sudden, we had improved margin. We were fast with an answer and fast with a solution.

We infused our operations with business sense. We set up our bank to have a board of directors, something we would repeat for each branch location. But instead of stocking the boards with bankers, we filled them with businesspeople. And because of that, we ran our bank like a business. Mark Twain Bank had a similar model.

At the beginning of the Allegiant days, everything had a small-town feel to it. One of our new directors, Siggy, ran a supermarket. When the board members drank martinis, Siggy would take out his glass eyeball and put it in his glass.

I hated the small-town scene. I had bigger dreams beyond glass-eye martinis and secret Masonic temple rooms.

It's amazing to me how things fell into place by default. The Kahoka bank started making some money, and the following year, I learned that the North St. Louis Trust Company was for sale. The bank happened to be located in the lowest-income census tract in the city of St. Louis. But even so, it was a chance to work my way back in.

I found that opportunity in February 1990, and we closed on August 30. We took our $33 million bank in Kahoka and our $11 million bank in St. Louis, grew them a little bit, and next thing we knew, we had a $51 million bank.

Our first two banks offered a good training ground. Businesspeople wouldn't visit our St. Louis location because they didn't feel safe. North St. Louis experienced its highest murder rate in 1990 and 1991. We would interview women and offer them jobs, and on their first day they wouldn't show up. We'd call them to find out what happened. "My husband won't let me work there." The location posed a huge challenge. But we were small and hungry, so we figured it out.

We shifted to banking on the go. We'd call a client and say, "We will be at your office in an hour and a half with the documents." If their wife had to sign, too, we would coordinate. "Can she meet at the school parking lot at 12:45?" We created a culture of service and caring and getting stuff done. If people weren't interested in visiting our banks, we needed to be able to meet them wherever they were. We couldn't sit back and wait for people to show up like UMB with its ritzy corporate dining room.

Our operations in the days before widespread cell phone usage became a series of meetings in easy-to-reach parking lots. McDonald's was a favorite. "Take exit seven off of I-64. There's a McDonald's there. I'll meet you in the back." I knew every street in St. Louis.

I had a Brother typewriter in the trunk of my LeSabre (it was good at holding things other than cash), and if you needed a loan, I might walk out to the car, get the typewriter, and type out a note to make a deal with you.

I was also listed in the white pages. I didn't have caller ID, and if I was at home, I answered my phone. A customer called me up one time from a cruise ship wanting to buy a house. "Lee, we'll do it, no problem," I told him. But I charged him an extra $5,000 fee because he called me on Sunday afternoon. He paid it without flinching. He wanted to be able to go to dinner that night with his wife and say, "Honey, we got the house." A few weeks later, my phone bill came in, and instead of the normal $46, it was $246, so I sent him a bill for $200.

Banking meant service, and service meant discretion. I became the holder of secrets.

I was invited to an office building one day, and a woman came from behind the desk and handed me a nondisclosure, non-solicit confidentiality form—a good one. I signed the form, and we went inside.

"Shaun, you don't know me, but we both have kids at Country Day who are about ten years apart. You signed a confidentiality agreement, and if you violate it, I will make your life an absolute, total, unequivocal living hell."

"Okay. I've signed a few before. So, what are we getting down to?"

"My brother and I own a 900-number service. And no one knows what we do. We have these beautiful offices here in St. Louis where we do accounting and stuff like that. But out in Los Angeles we have women talking to men on the phone. We do about twelve-million dollars a year. Our problem is, about four million gets charged back. And we're trying to figure out how to improve our margin."

"This is not something that I can help you with," I told them. Not for any moral reason, but because it wasn't an area of expertise. We didn't care what kind of business you were in. There were no moral judgments. We were simply interested in getting your business.

We made sure to focus our attention on the things that mattered. And making our banks look nice was not a main focus. Marvin Wool had worked in various industries, one of which included the carpet-backing business, and one time he swung us a deal: seaweed green carpeting for one dollar a square yard. Guess what our branches looked like? A kelp forest. We bought a trailer-truck load of Marvin's carpet.

But while we were papering over some of the aesthetic issues at our banks, friction was building between me and Mike. I went home depressed from work one day and told my wife, "I can't believe that Mike can't make a decision." I learned that no decision *was* a decision—that inaction comes with its own consequences. I committed to making a decision, whether right or wrong, and to learn from that decision.

The reality was, he was all but retired. He'd completely checked out as soon as we got this thing going. There were nine directors on the board, and though I only brought on two of them, I'd also raised well over half the money. I drove 168 miles the wrong way each day, raising the money through people I didn't know. Mike Cole was like, "Okay, we're done. It'll all work." But this wasn't going to work without hard work, and Mike wasn't interested in it. That left me to do the work by myself.

Mike Cole was not looking out for the shareholder and not being a good steward.

Then came the Malcolm Cheek fiasco. I met Malcolm, then the president of the engineering firm Y&A Group, during my UMB days. He wrote a $50,000 check in our first meeting after I joined Allegiant. Another time, he gave Mike and me a stock tip at lunch. We each bought 1,000 shares and made $2,000 to $3,000 in a day before dumping the stock. In short order, we invited Malcolm to join Allegiant's board.

What Malcolm really wanted to do was borrow money for himself and his friends. Of course, we got sucked right into that.

Malcolm borrowed lots of money from Allegiant and about a dozen other Missouri banks. Then, in 1991, he disappeared. He had masterminded a massive pump-and-dump scheme that involved faking his death, going on the run for three years, living in rural Georgia, and selling log homes under a different name before he was captured in 1994.

The Malcolm Cheek situation brought FBI attention, and it highlighted the result of trusting the wrong person.

It all reminded me of my dealings with bank regulators—the same tone, the same tenor, the same demeanor. The regulators show up and look through your documents and statements trying to find *anything*.

Pretty quickly, I developed a technique for dealing with regulators. I had my lieutenants deal with them every day since they'd be in for two or three weeks. And then at the end, they dealt with me. I was constantly keeping score. I kept tabs on the things they were asking for and the concessions I might have to make. Every night when they went home, we strategized. *If we have to sacrifice somebody, who are we sacrificing?* There was a methodology. This was battle.

Damage control was an art form.

We ended up losing money in 1991 due to Malcolm Cheek. We could have made $50,000 with some sharper accounting. But if accounting had buried that issue, my frustrations with Mike— that he wasn't driven or committed to contribute to the bank's success—might not have bubbled over.

Mike's inaction frustrated me, but it also helped me develop my abilities and better understand the other areas of a bank.

The business world is a ruthless, unforgiving place, especially when people's money is at stake. The power seduced me, and I was hooked. I liked that people needed my help. People called me *The Godfather*, and sometimes *The Godfather* has to turn on someone close to him—someone who'd helped them in the past.

Which was what happened when Marvin Wool came to me one day.

"You know the wrong guy is running this," he told me.

"Well, I believe that, but there's nothing I can do," I said.

"We're gonna figure it out."

We went to very good corporate lawyers in St. Louis and told them the quandary, how Mike Cole wasn't working out.

"The directors will support Shaun," Marvin explained.

"No problem. Here's what we're going to do. We're going to draft a resolution at the board meeting next Wednesday that says Mike Cole is out as CEO. There are nine spots, and you've got six people who will sign," a lawyer told us. "Go get your six people to sign. On Monday, you guys will meet with Mike Cole and show him this sheet of paper. *But do not give it to him.* You're just showing it to him. See, there's nine spots, we already have six votes. You've lost."

This was the Ides of March 1992. When Mike came in and saw those six signatures, he immediately stormed out and went to one of his closest colleagues on the board, who capitulated.

That potentially shifted the balance from five to four.

We reached out to one female board member who joined our camp, putting us back at six votes. Within a few hours, we were up seven votes to two.

But there was an issue. This vote counting wasn't official. A director can only technically vote in a qualified meeting—meaning there was no teeth in our piece of paper.

We didn't do anything illegal. But we did push every button

we could. We hired the best and biggest lawyers and said, "Don't tell me I can't do something. Tell me how I can do it, and then I'll figure out if it's worth the aggravation."

We were gunslinging businessmen with a bank charter, and nothing was going to stop us.

CHAPTER 4
FATHER AND SON

I wish I had known my father before the light went out.

Paul Hayes came from a family of six. He grew up during the Great Depression in Oklahoma. It was a hard life. His dad, Clyde, was a fighter and fire-and-brimstone religious. They would go to church from eight o'clock in the morning to eight o'clock at night on Sundays.

Paul was the oldest and was protective of his siblings—especially his brother Clifford, who was five years younger.

When Paul got married to my mother Valerie Shipp in July 1941, Clifford was his best man. Paul had been in the ROTC and was destined for the Army Air Corps, but as a pilot, he feared he wouldn't survive the war. After the attack on Pearl Harbor, he got in his car and drove with another of his brothers, Eldon, to San Diego to join the Navy.

They both made it through the war, and my sister Candy came along in 1946. My mom was almost 27 years old when Candy was born and my dad was 29, which was late to start a family back then. My parents were too busy for any more children for a while, as they spent their time running a hardware store, a motel, and then a restaurant.

Uncle Clifford, meanwhile, went to dental school, became a surgeon, and eventually started a practice in California. He went on a boondoggle fishing trip to Acapulco in 1955, and as he departed, his plane crashed into a mountain, killing him and 25 others. It was the worst air disaster in Mexico's history up to that point.

Clifford's death crushed my father. All of his success went to neutral. By the time I came along a few years later, there was this cloud of sadness hanging over everything.

My sister got to experience more of the good times. Before I was born, she and my parents traveled to Florida around Christmastime and stayed there for a few months. My sister would be enrolled in school for the winter quarter.

The trips to Florida allowed my dad to race speedboats. He was a world champion three years in a row. The trophies are stored away. It was a labor of love for him, but it was also a rich man's sport, and we didn't have rich man's money—even with the safes in our house.

When the money dried up with speedboat racing, my father raced quarter horses. One time when I was about eight years old, my father took me to the track with him. He had a match race challenge with another horse owner, and the winner take home was $1,000. My father knew the other guy was juicing his horse up, so instead of going out right at four o'clock at the time of the race, he stayed an extra 10 minutes so the other horse's drugs would wear off. Right before we walked our horse down to the track, my father gave his horse a shot. Paul took his horse out and smoked the other guy's horse.

My mother, meanwhile, would wake up some days and say, "We're going to the Cardinals game today." We'd get four-dollar box seats at Busch Stadium, and I was in heaven.

My childhood was screwy. How many kids work at a motel? I rented rooms before I was 10 years old. If you were commercial, it was $7.21, and for individuals it was $9.27. No wonder I'm so good at math! The businesspeople who came every week got a discount. I wasn't big enough to make a bed, but I could strip them and carry towels to rooms. I later worked in the restaurant my parents owned.

I was the only kid I knew in Thayer whose parents went to college. My parents were on an older track than the parents of my childhood friends. My dad was a World War II veteran. My classmates' dads served in Korea.

My mom and dad had a bitter relationship. They would've gotten divorced by today's standards, but people didn't do that back then. They stuck with each other even though they didn't have the emotional patience to love each other anymore.

My father was intense—everyone was afraid of him. Including me. He wasn't someone you messed with. But he was also supportive of me, and as I entered college and the working world, he and I became closer.

When I was 30 years old (this would have been right around 1990 after we opened Allegiant), I went back to Thayer and we spent a day together.

Father and son. Man to man.

It was cleansing and turned out to be the perfect day. We said everything that needed to be said to each other.

My father died a few years later, and I'm forever grateful that we were able to make our peace. Thinking back on that day gives me hope that I can one day reconcile with my own children before it's too late. I want them to know how sorry I am for the pain that I caused them.

CHAPTER 5
PUSHING AND PUSHING AND PUSHING

Being overdrawn at the Fed seven days in a row might as well have meant the end of the world.

Or the end of Allegiant.

We had stretched ourselves thin and *needed* money—we couldn't be overdrawn another day. I didn't have a trunk-full of cash in my LeSabre to drop off this time. Instead, I stood in St. Louis Lambert International Airport with a fellow bank executive named Bill awaiting the arrival of his business partner—a potential loan buyer. But his flight was late.

The clock was ticking. Time was money, and money was everything.

"Bill, I need you to wire a quarter million dollars," I pleaded.

"Shaun, if Bob were here, I know he'd say, 'do it,' but I gotta wait for Bob's permission." Bob, the potential loan buyer on the late flight, was a state rep who knew nothing about banking. He did, however, buy a Pizza Hut franchise in 1965 that made him $20,000 a month. Money meant nothing to him. And now we needed his help.

"Bill, you dumb motherfucker!" I yelled. "The Federal Reserve is going to close me today if I'm overdrawn again. You'd better wire the quarter million dollars!"

The bank got the money and stayed afloat. That was the intensity that brewed inside of me—the same intensity that had brewed inside my father. Intensity would fuel my rise and expedite my downfall. I was intoxicated by the rush and risk, the power and ego that goes along with running a *real bank*. This is what I felt that we'd became by the end of 1993 when we crossed $100 million in total assets for the first time.

It was a major milestone. Lots of banks don't get that big.

My own wealth was growing, too. Between my real estate wealth and bank investments, I became a millionaire by the time I was 32.

Allegiant was steadily expanding strategically. We added two banks in 1992, which was the same year my twins Brooks and Ryan were born. Additional locations followed in the years ahead. By infusing business sense into our operations, we grew 30% year over year. We went from $68 million at the end of 1992 to passing $100 million in 1993. In 1994, we passed $171 million.

Our growth expanded further after I spent eight months trying to buy the troubled Missouri State Bank in downtown St. Louis. It meant I spent a ton of time helping the bank work through some problem loans, learning skills I might not have encountered otherwise. That experience connected me with Jim Wilkson—a genius at bank operating systems and IT.

Allegiant hired Jim to run its IT operations, and we made our first major investment in technology by spending $400,000. Jim was an early adopter, and our focus on technology and automation transformed our company. We stopped automatically sending bank statements or checks and instead began pushing debit cards. You walked into a bank and left with a debit card.

We didn't want customers writing a check—checks cost us money because of the time and manpower needed to process them. Debit transactions, which required nothing of us, were *making* us money.

We automated, centralized, and streamlined our processes. We had a central call center for a *farshtunken* little bank at a time when no one else did. You'd call 314-692-8200 and reach someone who would say, "Allegiant Bank, how may I help you?" If you called a typical branch for another bank, you'd talk to a branch receptionist who would connect you with someone else, and that other person would transfer you to someone else. We were way out there, and I give all the credit to my management.

Our technological changes became a cost differentiator for us and allowed us to scale without adding workforce. We could do a lot of things with technology because we weren't stuck in an old business model. We didn't have legacy expenses or the burden of big computer banks for check processing.

In large part because of our IT efforts, we were able to expand from two to fourteen branches over the course of six years. We were eating up geography. My business cards featured a map on the back with dots showing our locations. I gave away tons of those business cards. We wanted to show people that we were more than just a mom-and-pop bank.

Guiding a bank required shrewdness. I wasn't interested in throwing money at every trivial thing, like designing a company logo. How could we represent *Allegiant* as a symbol? AT&T had come out with a logo showing the world with lines in it, so Allegiant's logo became a triangle with lines in it. Some may call it plagiarism, but I thought of it as "inspired by." AT&T probably spent a fortune on their logo. We got ours for free.

Another time when I was vacationing in Florida, I saw an ad in the newspaper for a 16-month CD (certificate of deposit). I was always interested in oddball promotions, and I liked this one. I cut the ad out of the newspaper, brought it home with me, and gave it to our ad guy. I wanted us to run a similar promotion. A week later I picked up the St. Louis Post-Dispatch and saw our ad with the same month-old start date listed as the ad in the Florida paper. I guess we copied a little too closely on that one.

You name it, we tried it. We were driven by the almighty dollar and the almighty deal. Marvin Wool, who took over as Allegiant's chairman from Mike Cole, taught me an important lesson: don't be afraid to ask—all someone can do is say no. When he traveled, he was cheaper than cheap. When he needed some new luggage, he went into the Famous-Barr department store, which became a Macy's.

"What are you gonna give me that's not on sale?" Marvin asked the salesman, who would take the next smallest piece and put it inside and sell it to him. Who would even think to ask for a discount at a department store? I didn't before meeting Marvin. But he was looking for discounts and handouts at every turn, and that mindset rubbed off on me.

I typically wore Bass Weejuns loafers, which cost about $175. Every spring they were on sale. I would go to Dillard's and Famous-Barr in the same mall and haggle with the salesmen since both stores sold them.

"What kind of deal can you give me?" I'd ask the Famous-Barr salesperson.

"I can't do anything. They're on sale."

"Okay. I'm going to Dillard's."

"Alright, wait, wait, wait!" The salesperson would come back, and my shoes would each have free shoe trees in them.

Marvin was always thinking two steps ahead. One example is when it came to commitment letters for bids. Our commitment letters were typically four pages long—pages two, three, and four were boilerplate. But we might create six different page ones. Marvin was used to the bidding process from the time he spent in the chemical business.

When the bids were due, he would tap his jacket. "I got my bid here in my coat pocket—I can't change it." He'd have different letters in both breast pockets, in his side pockets, and in his hip pockets.

The bid would come in at 37 and a half cents. "Son of a gun!" And he'd reach into the pocket that had the 37 and a quarter.

We were always looking for add-ons, even when it came to the loans we granted. We would jockey against other banks and justify the extra cost. *Isn't it worth $408.33 a month to have my home number, my cell number, and my pager number?* Other bankers held banker's hours, rolling into work at nine a.m., leaving early to head to the golf course. I didn't golf. And my mornings started with *early* meetings, just as they had in my days of back-to-back breakfasts.

An equipment company owner gave us a nice plug in the *St. Louis Business Journal,* talking about all of the banks that had turned them down (I think it was 42), and how Allegiant lent them the money to grow their business. What he didn't tell was that we had an investor put up a million dollars. None of these other banks had the balls to ask. We had the reputation of taking on a ton of risk. But we had very few problem loans, and we took chances that were bound to pay off. We did stuff that other banks didn't do. We would ask and wind up with 5% ownership of the company. We would find a way to get something, and that would improve our yield and reduce our risk. We asked for the things that UMB would have never asked.

We weren't doing anything illegal. We were just pushing.

And pushing.

And pushing.

There was this restaurant that made the best spicy chicken sandwiches and pizza. On Tuesday nights, kids ate free. They had previously worked with another bank, but they were down, and we lent them money. The owners came in one day.

"Shaun, the other bank wants us back, and they'll lower our rate."

Ugh. I looked at the owners and said, "Here's the deal guys. If you walk out the door, don't ever come back." It pissed me off. I really liked their Cajun chicken sandwich!

About six months later, they did come crawling back. And guess what I said? "Fuck off and die."

We went public on the NASDAQ in September 1995 under the symbol ALLE. We had 338 shareholders. Marvin owned 14% of the company, making him the largest shareholder, and I was the next largest shareholder at 7 or 8%. It was exciting to have money of my own, even if a lot of it was tied up in Allegiant. But when your goal is to have money, you just want more. You want the pile to grow.

Nothing was enough.

The *St. Louis Post-Dispatch* profiled our bank on October 17, 1995, under the headline, "Loan Ranger: Business Executive

Builds Bank Chain," and I was pictured with Marvin, all smiles. Our relationship was all about money—it wasn't a friendship. Marvin always wanted things to be about him, and the article was his validation. Me? I didn't care about the personal credit—leave the credit and newspaper coverage to the Marvin Wools and Crosby Kempers. I simply wanted respect for our not-so-little bank. I wanted people to pay attention to what we were doing.

People like Denis O'Brien, a St. Louis native whose dad was president of Ralston Purina. Denis also happened to be a business manager for Beatles musician George Harrison.

One day in 1996 when Allegiant was a $400 million bank, Denis asked me to lunch. We met and Denis droned on and on about George even though I didn't give a flying fuck about George Harrison. Finally, after an hour of talking, Denis got to the point of the meeting. "Shaun, we want to buy your bank."

This is when, for me, the tables turned, and the power trip went from 7 to 700.

"Okay Denis, it's for sale. I'll get you the information, and you have to sign a nondisclosure confidentiality. Have you done any research?"

"No, why would I?"

"Because we're four times the size of your bank."

There was nothing that matched up to that moment. This guy spent an hour blabbing about George Harrison, and the entire time, I waited like a poker player with pocket aces for the perfect time to strike. He didn't even belong at my table. That's how much of a son of a bitch I had become. The power, success, and ego had changed me.

My ego and our bank were growing too fast to maintain. It didn't help when Jim Wilkson, our IT guru, left in 1995. Jim's deputy, Ray, stepped up to run the department, but he wasn't adequate. It took a full year to hire Kim Palmer to lead our IT efforts. We also made an even bigger investment in technology to the tune of $1.7 million. But there was a steep learning curve, and training took time. I made a promise that we wouldn't buy anything until our new infrastructure was in place.

But I didn't stick to that promise.

We used our stock to make an acquisition in the spring of 1997. Reliance Federal Savings and Loan in south St. Louis County was a $30 million bank. Kim reminded me of my vow not to buy anything, so we decided to keep the S&L as a separate subsidiary and didn't merge it into Allegiant's operations until 1998, which solved that problem.

We also borrowed $75 million on a short-term basis to fund our growth, which wasn't something that regulators liked since it's not a sound strategy. Mercantile was divesting of banks in Warrenton and Union, Missouri. Those were two markets we wanted to enter, and so against Kim's sound advice not to buy any more banks, we became aggressive bidders.

Those banks had a large volume of accounts, and 25% of our

total deposits meant more volume than the other 75% of the deposits we had because we didn't have many transaction accounts.

We won the bid by the end of May and had to convert the banks to Allegiant on Labor Day weekend.

Being the optimist I am, I said, "We'll figure out a way to make this work." When you buy a bank from another bank, you buy their deposits—meaning we had $80 million in deposits coming into the purchase. We were like drug addicts waiting for that wire transfer to clear. We needed that to go through so we wouldn't have to owe the Fed any money. That pesky Federal Reserve.

The deposits could solve our liquidity problem. Kim—who was pregnant at the time—was (rightfully) in a state of panic. We merged in Warrenton and Union on Labor Day weekend in 1997 using our current system.

The banks shut down at two o'clock to process everything and make the switch. Normally we'd be done by six or seven at night. It wasn't done until noon the next day.

To make matters worse, there was an error. If you went to an Allegiant ATM or branch to cash your check or take out money during that adjustment period, we didn't charge your account. We were simply giving out free money.

We didn't figure out the problem until we had lost $1,547,000.

That Monday, I was beside myself. I sat in my car outside of my son's school before a parent-teacher conference screaming into the phone.

"Just fire somebody!" I yelled, as I punched the steering wheel of my Lincoln Continental. I might as well have gone 15 rounds with that steering wheel. I pushed everyone to the brink. But despite all the pushing, the growth, and the IT upgrades, we hadn't made the necessary investments in accounting.

When you're a $600 million- bank, you have to act like one. We were operating on such thin numbers, and it came back to bite us.

At the time, I considered it my biggest failure. And yet, we ended with a record year. Outside of a few people inside the bank, no one knew that we pissed away $1.5 million. Our earnings were up 25%! There were no real consequences, which only empowered me further.

CHAPTER 6
THERMONUCLEAR WAR

Losing $1.5 million is a pretty good motivator to make changes.

The struggles Allegiant encountered, such as the money we flushed away on Labor Day weekend in 1997, reinforced the need for us to establish more structures and safeguards. The screw-ups were costing us real money.

The bank buckled down on accounting and changed firms to Ernst & Young. They were expensive—upward of $500,000 a year—but their tax advice not only paid for the increased cost, but it also made us sharper and more decisive in running the company.

We also made some tough decisions about the bank's direction. During the 1990s, we had focused on growing a big footprint, and I had a map put on the back of my business cards showing our branch locations. Kahoka was Allegiant's first bank in 1989. Acquiring it helped us lay the foundation for our journey, but our focus shifted to St. Louis, and keeping a branch 168 miles away didn't seem like a smart decision.

The Northeast Missouri operation just wasn't in our plans anymore. We sold the Kahoka branch along with branches in Palmyra and Monroe City. I'd stopped making the trips to Kahoka years earlier, but losing Kahoka was a symbolic move. We were turning the page on Allegiant's past and looking ahead to the future. Selling those assets also helped us pare and restructure our balance sheet.

We scrutinized every aspect of our company, and one piece *scared* me. Edge Mortgage Services was a subprime lender that provided loans for lenders who struggled to get approved elsewhere. We even advertised it in the newspaper. "When you're living on the edge, call Edge Mortgage."

If my days at UMB taught me anything about *good conservative banking*, it was that subprime lending was a path to disaster. What if the market softened? What if there was a recession? Subprime lending carried too much risk, and running a bank was all about increasing control and minimizing risk.

I was so scared about subprime lending that I gave Edge Mortgage away. We sold it for $25,000—$1,000 down and a $24,000 note. I told the buyer I didn't care if they made any additional payments. They never did.

I was also dabbling in personal real estate deals at the time, too. One of the most promising ones involved the intersection of McKnight and Manchester in the St. Louis suburb of Rock Hill. I-64 is to the west, 61 is north, and the intersection of these two roads represented a growth opportunity.

I lived nearby, and in 1997, Michael Litz—a real estate developer who I was friendly with—approached me with the idea of buying a dry cleaner at the intersection together. I'd connected with Mike through his brother, a sharp-as-an-arrow attorney.

Mike had long gray hair and didn't get married until his 40s. He held the ceremony in his home with a horse in attendance. Extremely smart and gregarious, Mike loved wine and food.

He developed a limited liability company, McKnight Man LLC, for our real estate ventures, and we got a loan to cover the purchase of the dry cleaner. We'd invest in properties here and there.

Mike ended up buying a few dozen houses nearby as part of a subdivision that went to the site of an old quarry. A few years later, we bought adjacent strip mall land through our LLC.

Michael was a pro. I had no reason to question things.

As Allegiant faced upheaval and I built my investment portfolio, my personal life went through a rough patch. My mother died in 1998, and even though we had our struggles, the loss unmoored me. My parents were both gone.

Change is constant. But sometimes change catches you by surprise, as it did on February 12, 1999, when my mobile phone rang. It was my wife, Sandra. She didn't normally call me at work.

"Come home now," she told me. I was worried that one of the kids was hurt. The boys, thankfully, were fine. But Sandra wasn't.

She wasn't happy in our marriage anymore.

Her announcement stunned me. I thought that we would *make it*—we gave off the aura of a perfect couple. But Sandra had sold her business a few years earlier, and our lives were drifting in different directions. I was so focused on success that I didn't give her what she needed.

We tried to fix things. I went to therapy twice a week. I had to get my act together—if not for myself or for our marriage, then as the leader of the company. I needed an outlet to get out all of the bitterness and disappointment. My therapist told me something prophetic: "You're going to implode in ten years." What did he know? I brushed the comment aside. But as I learned later, he was exactly right. I was wound too tight. And a person can only be wound so tight for so long.

Therapy couldn't save the marriage. Even though half of marriages end in divorce, I was blindsided when it happened to me. *Failure.* Maybe I took the marriage for granted. Maybe I was too focused on the company. I dunno. My job demanded power and control, and yet I had none of those things at home.

We sat down and divided everything. It was all very businesslike. I kept the house and took the bulk of the custody since it was the least disruptive arrangement for the children. The boys were 11 and 6 at the time, and it was their time to be with dad. Despite the arrangement, I knew I had to find someone and couldn't raise them alone.

Instead of me taking the time to regroup, losing Sandra fueled my competitive drive. I needed to find someone new, *now.* Both my sister-in-law and my lawyer had women lined up. I was a commodity—young, fit, and rich, and a good dad to boot.

It wasn't long before I met Kelly. She was valedictorian in high school, summa cum laude at St. Louis University, and top of her Washington University law school class. She was 35 and had never been married. We moved fast. Our relationship quickly spurred a proposal, then a marriage, and soon enough, we were having a set of twins—Paige and Jack—to go along with my three older children. Kelly is a great mother.

It was a season for matchmaking and new beginnings. At the same time my marriage to Sandra was ending and I began dating Kelly, our bank began looking for a new CFO. The outgoing CFO thought her lieutenant should replace her (I didn't agree). Four or five board members thought they had the right person selected, too.

Tom Daiber wrote me a letter expressing interest in the position. Tom ran our loan review. He wasn't your typical big-talking, look-you-in-the-eyes bank executive. He was quiet and withdrawn. While I dressed in designer clothes, Tom often looked like he had slept in his clothes.

Be that as it may, the more I thought about Tom, the more I recognized he had the skills to be a great CFO. He saw problems and opportunities from many angles. He was brilliant. I talked about it with Virginia Kirkpatrick, a longtime, loyal member of our board of directors.

"I think he's the guy," she said.

"I do too," I said.

It took a little bit of politicking to get him past the board because they thought of him as Tom the quiet loan review guy. Eventually I won them over. Tom's quiet demeanor was the perfect fit for Allegiant's style. With banks and other companies, when you have three or four people talking as mouthpieces, the message gets diluted. Everything flowed between Tom and I, but he wasn't interested in taking the limelight for himself.

The first order of business? Taking Tom suit shopping. I also gave him some of my Ferragamo ties, and he still wears them.

Another key hire was Jeff Schatz as our *chief of operations*, not chief operating officer. Notice the difference? Jeff had previously guided Sky Bank out of Ohio and has family in St. Louis. Jeff was sharp. With his hiring, IT wound up reporting to him.

The titles and selective hiring were a reflection of our board, which was as selfish as it was protective of me. Marvin Wool wanted to maintain his power as chairman of the board, and hiring a chief operating officer would have certainly diminished his power. Additionally, we had already been through a power struggle in the Mike Cole situation. We didn't need to bring in another bigwig from some other bank only to have them turn around and try to knock me off. Most banks handed out titles. Everybody at Mark Twain was a president. Not Allegiant. We had one president: me.

Under Tom's guidance and by using our bulked-up accounting resources, we issued our first "trust-preferred security," a type of debt instrument that counted as capital for government purposes but was tax deductible as a dead instrument. We issued $10 million that traded on the stock exchange.

While our common stock had been listed on the NASDAQ for four years, this was new and different. We were taking advantage of the opportunities available to us instead of simply reacting. First Union, one of the country's largest banks, put a small syndicate together. I did a roadshow, and we sold out in one day. For me, that moment marked a transformation. We weren't just some community bank anymore. We were thriving and had crossed the $750 million threshold. Three-quarters of a billion dollars.

I was in my element and having fun.

But there was a problem on the horizon. Y2K was an anticipated computer programming glitch that was poised to potentially bring down computer systems worldwide when the year switched from 1999 to 2000.

Other banking leaders were panicking about Y2K. I spoke to an executive with the brokerage firm A.G. Edwards about it during a social meet-up at a country club near my house, and it was all he wanted to talk about.

"Every two weeks we get paid, you know what I do? I take $500 in cash and hide it," he told me. This guy worked at one of the largest investment banks in the country, and he was *stashing cash* because he was worried the world was going to end.

There was being prepared. Our bank certainly was, but whether anything happened was not something I spent time worrying about. The bank examiners and government regulators kept close tabs on everything with test runs and reports.

On New Year's Eve, December 31, 1999, Kelly and I went to dinner at Morton's and got home after midnight. *The sky wasn't falling.* I hopped on the phone and checked in with our IT team. Out of 140,000 accounts, we had about 400 accounts with issues, but no money lost. We prepared for Armageddon, but in the end, everything turned out to be clear skies—a recurring theme for Allegiant in 2000. One of our biggest successes was a partnership with the NFL's St. Louis Rams, the defending Super Bowl champions. The Rams came calling to see how Allegiant could partner with them, and as a rabid sports fan, I thought a Rams partnership could take us to another level of visibility.

With sports teams, lots of companies fall over themselves to become corporate sponsors. But what good is it to sponsor a box or something else so frivolous? No, if we were going to sponsor something, I wanted it to pay off.

We reached a five-year deal to become the official bank of the Rams. That meant Allegiant's logo on the Trans World Dome scoreboards and our ATM machines throughout the stadium. Our little bank's logo alongside Budweiser and Pepsi.

Our profile was growing, and our infrastructure and accounting were in place. We found ourselves with a golden opportunity to scale our bank. Tom Daiber's accounting work opened the door for us to buy Equality Savings Bank (which had about $300 million in assets) in late 2000 with low capital and without us having to raise equity. We bought the bank with our stock and suffered minimal dilution. After it was complete, we were able to enhance our earnings per share.

Between our bolstered accounting efforts and Rams partnership and acquisitions, we were on track for our best year yet. On November 15, 2000, we crossed an elusive barrier: one billion in assets. In less than eight years, we had grown 22-fold.

We had our sights on growing larger still. Mergers and acquisitions were the most effective way to grow, and they were happening at a record pace in the 1990s and early 2000s as baby boomer bank executives reached their 50s and wanted to cash out. Despite all the talk about shareholders, the main focus with mergers and acquisitions is lining the pockets of the management. Basically, it was human greed.

Greed was fueling our growth effort, too. We spoke to dozens of banks each year about acquiring them, and we were often told "no." But Southside—which had 16 locations and $750 million in total assets—stood out to us. We tried to acquire them the year before, but the CEO declined to have any meaningful discussions with Allegiant.

Allegiant had 23 locations and was worth $1.1 billion at the time. A merger was poised to take our assets near $2 billion and make us the fifth-largest bank in St. Louis—with a big gap between the smaller banks and us.

Tom Daiber walked into my office one day. "I've been working on the numbers, Shaun. We can buy Southside," he told me. At the time, they were trading for around eight dollars a share. "I know there's a deal to be made here, but you're going to have to do it," he said.

An issue with Southside involved Jim Dierberg, who owned First Banks. He was the largest shareholder of Southside at nearly 25%, but the government, due to regulatory ownership requirements, wouldn't allow him control over management or decision-making. This lack of control frustrated Jim, as he was a quite successful and powerful man.

I called the CEO of Southside again. "Hey, we talked a year ago about a possible sale, but it didn't go anywhere. Would you have any interest now?" I asked. We spent about half an hour on the phone going through the numbers. Resistant but cordial, he ended the call with another rejection. *No thanks.*

Tom reminded me that I knew one of the directors and a large shareholder, Doug Helein, through a previous attempt to buy the Central West End Savings and Loan four years earlier. So, I picked up the phone and called Doug. I outlined the fact that we could pay $10 a share for Southside.

He dropped the phone on his desk and it about burst my eardrum. He picked up the phone and apologized. He was shaking and could hardly speak.

"Shaun, let me make some phone calls," he said. "We'd do anything to get out of this investment, and the CEO only wants to protect his job. I can't believe you didn't talk to me a year ago." *Sometimes it's not enough to ask—you need to ask the right person.*

Doug called me back about 20 minutes later. "Norville McClain, who is a non-employee chairman of the board, is in Florida and will call you at exactly four o'clock," Doug told me.

Tom and I waited, and sure enough, Mr. McClain called. He could not have been more gracious, explaining the parameters and restrictions of who we should and shouldn't talk to. He also said we should avoid speaking to Jim Dierberg, who wasn't allowed to be an officer or director because of his controlling interest in another bank. The directors wanted to do a deal, and after Norville flew back from Florida, we would meet the following Monday and sign the necessary agreements formally barring us from communicating with Jim.

But until that paperwork was signed, those directives were only suggestions—which is why Tom and I met with Jim Dierberg's attorneys the next day on a Saturday. He was the largest shareholder, and someone whose presence could kill the deal.

Saturdays in downtown St. Louis are dead, and we were extra cautious. We went through the wrong building, parked in different places, and went up different elevators because Jim was paranoid. If anyone knew about this, we'd be in trouble.

Southside happened to have four charters: a St. Louis City Charter (the big bank), St. Charles County, Jefferson County, and St. Genevieve. If we did the deal straight-up, Dierberg would have owned 14%. My board would not have taken that. The Fed might not have taken it. He was already a two-billion-dollar bank, and that meant influence. Tom suggested giving Jim the banks in Jefferson, St. Charles, and St. Genevieve counties since it would be tax-free for him. We got our lawyers, and he had his lawyers. We weren't formally meeting and couldn't put anything in writing. But we wanted to be gentlemen about this and find a way to make this work for all parties.

After our clandestine correspondence with Dierberg, we signed the paperwork that Monday barring us from communicating with him further, and the merger talks intensified. Plans for the merger were announced in May of that year.

The following month, First Banks asked for the right to buy the three banks we had discussed, which Southside promptly derailed.

The deal moved forward and was poised to close at the end of September 2001. We planned to raise the necessary capital by issuing trust-preferred securities. We had a trip to Washington, D.C. scheduled for the week after Labor Day.

It was an exciting time for St. Louis. The city was hosting the PGA Tour's American Express Championship, and while I'm not a golfer, it was electric to watch Tiger Woods during his practice round on Monday, September 10. I planned to watch the tournament later that week after heading to Washington and other cities with Tom Daiber.

That Tuesday, the day of our trip, I awoke and was shaving when my wife called to me.

"Shaun, get in here."

A plane had slammed into the World Trade Center's north tower in New York City. I knew people in that building and had been there months earlier.

Something was horribly wrong. Was it an accident? Did the pilot have a heart attack?

The awful truth emerged minutes later when a second plane slammed into the World Trade Center's south tower. Other planes crashed in Washington and western Pennsylvania.

America was under attack.

The day was a flurry of uncertainty—phone calls, meetings, fear, panic, and many unknowns for the country and for my bank. Our trip to sell securities was off. Flights were grounded nationwide, and the financial markets were closed, too. Nobody was doing anything in the stock or bond markets.

It was a time to grieve. But I was focused on time. If we didn't close the Southside deal by the last business day of the month, we would incur a $10 million penalty, which would all but kill the merger. The last possible day we could finalize this was Friday, September 28. It took three days to settle securities sales, which meant we needed to lock this in by Tuesday, September 25.

In a matter of days, we had gone from not having any problems to having every problem. We were looking at every option of pulling this off.

As the deadline approached, I went thermonuclear war. This was all up to me. All of the training, the negotiating, the maneuvering, and the hustling was coming down to this. If I succeeded, my little bank would enter the top tier of St. Louis banks. If I failed, we might never become the big bank I'd strived for so long to become.

The gravity of how much everything had changed was stark. There were six people on our flight, and the National Guard was stationed *everywhere*. Instead of hitting a bunch of locations on my road trip, as we initially planned, I went to Chicago, sat in a conference room, and spent the day on speakerphone talking to all of the people I would have visited on the road trip.

With no one buying securities, I had concern that we might not get the money. Doubt crept in.

We ended up selling $25 million worth of securities. We needed $20 million, which gave us $5 million extra in capital and leverage. The deal locked in *hours* ahead of the deadline. It felt like winning the lottery. Legg Mason, our investment banker, told me that we were one of the first companies in America to sell a security after 9/11.

The merger was official. Allegiant was a *big* bank. There was no denying us anymore.

CHAPTER 7
THE SALE

What do you do after you climb a mountain?

The Southside acquisition took Allegiant to the pinnacle of St. Louis banks. But the journey was arduous, and we were *exhausted* when it was complete. I had 38 branches and hundreds of employees to account for now. Our first step was to integrate everything under the Allegiant brand and push the retail sales culture we implemented in 1998.

I worked to figure out how to move the needle as the banking landscape changed. Gone were the days when Allegiant's board wondered, "How can we squeeze the most out of any transaction?" When we were much smaller, each loan and agreement mattered to us. Now, with two billion in assets, it was just money on a pile.

In the early Allegiant years, I knew just about *everybody* who banked with us. It wasn't like that anymore. Along the way, banking stopped being a sport and a game. No one needs a godfather's blessing when your credit score is the factor that gets your loan approved. This is what became the standard in the late 1990s and early 2000s, especially after Fannie Mae and Freddie Mac started relying on FICO scores for mortgage applications.

With the focus on credit score and automation, banking became less personalized and less about power and control.

More than that, Allegiant's core group had been together for 10 years by this point, and it's hard to keep a group together for so long. Marvin Wool, Kevin Farrel, Virginia Kirkpatrick, Lee Wielansky, and Leon Felman had all been the key players on the board. Between bank board meetings, holding company board meetings, at least one executive committee meeting a month, and loan committees, we saw each other all the time. Eventually, we all wore on each other.

Things weren't the same anymore, and I was trying to get the feeling back.

Guardian Savings out of California was divesting out of the Midwest, and we bought those banks for pennies on the dollar and integrated them into our operations. We also scooped up Investment Counselors Inc., a St. Louis money management firm.

But further acquisition opportunities in the St. Louis market—where we had our geographical competitive advantage—had all but dried up for banks our size. The playbook that fueled our growth wouldn't work anymore.

We considered looking outside St. Louis, but by doing so, we ran the risk of diluting Allegiant's brand like we had done in the early 1990s. It was growth for growth's sake without deeper strategy or purpose. We sold off Kahoka and other branches because those small-town rural banks didn't offer growth opportunities.

After the Southside deal, Allegiant faced an identity crisis. We began to look like every other regional bank, resembling the also-rans we had passed over the past decade. We had to find a way to grow double-digit earnings as we'd done for years in order to keep investors happy. This put added stress and pressure on my shoulders.

You start getting into larger and larger deals, and now you're in competition with larger regional or national banks that can compete on price. Our advantage came with lending, where we were quick with an answer but had higher fees and interest rates.

The bigger banks could do the things that we could do. By expanding, our differentiating factors didn't set us apart anymore.

It reminds me of a great story I heard from one of my mentors at UMB, Mr. Huwalt, at the beginning of my career. He had a celebrated career at First National in Kansas City, Mercantile in St. Louis, and an Ohio bank in the late 1960s that allowed him to join UMB. When he was a boy, his dad was head of the second largest bank in Grand Island, Nebraska. When the family gathered for dinner, his dad would say, "Now, be sure and pray for the State Bank of Grand Island."

"Why?" the boy asked.

"Well, son, the First National Bank has the best borrowers with the best credit, and then when they get a ding or two, we get them. But we need a bank to send them when it deteriorates a little more, so we always pray for the state bank."

I prayed for a solution. The outcome that made the most sense was one we had flirted with for years, a path that banks like Mercantile, Magna, Mark Twain, and Southwest had already taken. Selling Allegiant was always the plan. Whenever I met with investment bankers, they told me, "Shaun, these five banks want to buy you." They were a lot like used car salesmen—they always had their sales book with them. They were never going to come in and say anything other than "the thing to do is sell."

Spending so much time working with a guy like Marvin Wool who bought and sold companies all the time got me predisposed to this process.

It might seem counterintuitive to acquire Southside and then turn around and pursue a sale, but keep this in mind: the Southside deal, more than size, maximized our shareholder value and drove up the potential payoffs for the board and other officers.

It was all about greed.

Allegiant's board and I both realized it would be advantageous to get out now instead of trying to hang on. I was proud to build Allegiant. Though it was the greatest success of my career, this wasn't some family legacy project like Crosby Kemper and UMB or a job I wanted to keep forever.

After spending a decade climbing the mountain, we were *tired,* and tired of each other. It seemed like we were all working on our exit strategies. Tom Daiber, who had been so instrumental during our growth years, came up with a plan.

"Shaun, we can personally buy the State Bank of Aviston in Illinois with a group of investors that I could put together." Tom grew up near Aviston in Highland, Illinois, so there was a personal connection for him.

I broached the plan with the board. They weren't fans of us buying a bank on the east side of the river *that wasn't Allegiant*, which I understood. This wasn't a big bank and bringing it under Allegiant's umbrella would have only complicated things. We had made a point to be geographically on brand and consistent. This way if we went to sell everything, it would be easy to operate for the incoming owner.

So Tom put a group together to buy the Aviston bank on his own. I agreed to invest some money as did others in the Allegiant family. When Tom announced he was leaving, Jeff Schatz was promoted to chief financial officer as well as chief operations officer. Jeff was bright and capable and had been with Allegiant for years.

It was bittersweet to lose Tom, though I was proud to see him following his own path.

In late 2002, we went to New York and Chicago to meet with investors. Tom, Jeff, and I were all together again. In one of the meetings, we spoke with a fund that had a position in a publicly traded bank in Kankakee, Illinois. Before the meeting was over, Tom and I arranged for discussions to merge the Illinois banks together—his $37 million Aviston bank would soon be a $300 million publicly traded savings and loan bank.

This was great for Tom, but it wouldn't mean much to us. If you're a capitalist dealing with billion-dollar mergers, what could you do with a $37 million suburban bank? It was a lot of effort for little payoff.

With our growth slowing, we made the tough decision to reduce our workforce. We ended up cutting 40 people in one day. We also instituted some other cost-cutting measures in order to streamline our operations, allowing us to be as lean as possible for a potential buyer.

We also needed capital.

Allegiant had never sold a share of common stock to the public, which was a source of personal pride. We used equity for the Reliance, Equality, and Southside acquisitions, but we never did an offering other than private placements.

Getting capital required us to go into promotional mode. We held a roadshow with investment bankers and spoke to them from a Chicago conference room. They ate up our story of success, our battles, our rise, the $750,000 in the trunk of the LeSabre, and our 11 years of growth. Jeff and I met with Legg Mason and came up with a plan to issue one million shares. It was capital that, when paired with our projected earnings, would keep us on track for an acquisition.

We executed the roadshow with perfection. If there was any doubt that Allegiant was a real bank, that went away when our stock was priced at over $17 a share in public sale. We wound up raising $17 million, giving us plenty of capital for what we had to accomplish. This was coupled with our $25 million in projected earnings after tax, less dividends.

The board needed to approve the pricing, and there was an issue. Since it was a Greenshoe (over-allotment) option, an extra 15% of company shares would be issued. Two of the board members adamantly opposed it. They didn't want to be diluted. Our investment banking team was confused. *How do these people not want this extra capital?*

The conference call with the board grew heated. I spent an hour on the phone with individual directors building support and getting consensus. It felt a little too much like Mike Cole's departure a decade earlier, but instead of negotiating with a winning hand, I was working from a disadvantage and was forced to beg and plead. Eventually enough board members came around, which allowed us to avoid looking like a bunch of amateurs. But it was one more nail in the proverbial coffin—another signal to sell.

But who would buy?

Bank of Montreal, which owned Harris Bank in Chicago, was interested in Allegiant, and I developed a relationship with the vice chairman. We had constant talks, discussions, and meetings, but nothing ever came of it.

Mick Aslin came calling, too. Mick, formerly of UMB, interviewed me before my banking career began, and ripped me when I resigned in 1989 (I knew it wasn't personal). Mick was a true competitor. After Mick left UMB—he was never going to be CEO because his last name wasn't Kemper—he later became the head of Gold Bank, which had grown into a five-billion-dollar bank with branches in Florida, Oklahoma, and Kansas. It was a nice-sized bank without a geographical strategy. Mick was there to give it credibility.

Mick invited me to visit Kansas City to talk. Little did I know that this would be the crowning moment of everything I had worked so hard for—the culmination of 20 years of hustle, sweat, and struggle. Over a long lunch, Mick proposed to merge Gold and Allegiant banks under the Allegiant name with headquarters in St. Louis. He would be chairman of the board and CEO, and I would be president. After one year, Mick would shift to non-executive chairman, and I would be the president and chief executive.

Wow.

Two decades after starting at UMB, I was on the cusp of running a UMB-sized bank. It was the ultimate ego boost.

But in my heart, I knew it wasn't right for the Allegiant shareholders. Shoehorning into an operation randomly spread across numerous states didn't make a lot of sense because it wouldn't lead to value creation.

It hurt to let that opportunity pass.

With conversations swirling, slow and methodical, it felt like we were all dressed up with nowhere to go. And then, in short order, we had two suitors vying for our affection.

The first was Associated Bank based in Green Bay, Wisconsin, that had about $10 billion in total assets. Associated wanted to grow and had a small presence with some savings and loans in St. Louis, so Allegiant appealed to them.

After Labor Day, Associated's CEO, Paul Biederman, came to St. Louis and spent the day with me. I knew they would not be the highest payer, but they were the kind of meat and potatoes bank you'd expect coming from Green Bay. Their culture was closer to UMB than Allegiant, which would be a tough transition for employees. Discussions between us were slow and methodical.

Then National City came calling. When Tim Lathe, a kind and personable exec at National City asked to meet, I didn't think much of it. The Cleveland-based bank was almost 50 times our size, with $100 billion in assets and 1,100 branches spread across Ohio, Illinois, Indiana, Kentucky, Michigan, and Pennsylvania. But they didn't have a presence in St. Louis.

We met, and in came the CEO along with Tim. I stuck my foot in my mouth immediately. "How was your flight?"

I didn't realize they had two company jets, including a new King Air. They had a fucking air force. Why did they need *us?* It was a different world having a $20 million jet pick you up and take you to Cleveland and get you back by dinnertime.

I kept our board's executive committee updated on this dance between our two potential partners. "I just don't see a $100 billion bank buying us," I said. I continued to think we would wind up selling to Associated Bank.

It sure seemed that way in November 2003 when Associated spent a week reviewing our loans and systems. We would be their biggest acquisition to date. Thankfully, we had excellent accounting and good risk-management practices. Everything was falling into place, and then National City reengaged. They'd heard we were nearing a deal with Associated Bank, and they offered to come to St. Louis that Friday and Saturday and do their due diligence.

The race was on!

National City came to town, and I looked to my executive committee for support. Marvin Wool, the consummate negotiator, told me, "Get the price up." The sales price was looking like it might be $26.50 or $26.75. At dinner that night, I made a list and told them everything that was wrong with Allegiant. I wanted to be forthright.

At the end of the night, they committed to pay $27 per share in cash or stock.

"We wanna do this deal," they said. That dinner netted Allegiant's shareholders an extra eight million dollars. Marvin was proud of me. National City had pulled ahead.

I traveled to Green Bay with Allegiant's leadership and investment bankers that following Monday for a day of negotiations with Associated Bank. We wanted to get a deal done, and the intent was to make a public announcement by the end of that week. The compartmentalizing and secrets and the weight of it all had worn on me.

We headed to the airport after a long day of meetings, and I called National City. "The contract is done," they said. I polled my most important board members. Yes. Yes. Yes!

The attorneys and investment bankers stalled Associated to make sure nothing bit us. I spoke to National City's next CEO, too. The only thing he said was the same criticism we always received. "Your branches need sprucing up." They looked like used car lots, but that wasn't something we cared about. And that would be up to National City to change.

I awoke the next morning, walked on the treadmill, and listened to CNBC. "Just in this morning. National City Bank, one of the country's largest banks, has acquired Allegiant Bancorp." I dressed, went to work, and found National City's CEO David Daberko in the office to meet Allegiant's senior staff.

The deal was done for $27.25 a share. I'd sold my little bank for *almost half a billion dollars*. It was the crowning achievement of my professional life. I had half a million shares of stock—nearly $14 million worth—along with a $2 million golden parachute. The stock was converted to National City stock.

I'd truly reached the mountaintop. And then I got lost.

CHAPTER 8
CALM BEFORE THE STORM

I loved making deals. It was my addiction, my rush, my high.

I thrived on the type of pressure I faced during my Allegiant days—the pressure that requires you to be constantly *on*. That type of pressure carried me through the months after we reached the deal to sell to National City.

After the deal was announced in late 2003, the work began to take a 38 bank, $2.5-billion operation and fold it into a behemoth. National City's people were smart and hardworking, and they could not have been more accommodating. But at the end of the day, we weren't even the tail of the dog—we were the tip of the tail. We fought so hard to build Allegiant into a real bank, but to National City, the acquisition came down to cost efficiencies and keeping things moving.

I relished the intellectual challenges of the transition. We tackled so many suggestions and hypotheticals about what to try and what not to try. So many issues to untangle. I was needed and felt important. It was a special time in my personal life, too. My wife, Kelly, gave birth to our twins, Paige and Jack, in February. Life was good.

The closing was set for April 9, 2004, which happened to coincide with a trip I took to watch my nephew Brandt Snedeker play in The Masters golf tournament at Augusta National. He was only an amateur player then, though a long and illustrious professional career would follow.

We couldn't take cell phones on the course. But I had an important call to make. I walked the grounds looking for a payphone, and at 11 a.m. eastern, I found one and called my attorney.

"The deal is done," my attorney told me. Allegiant was no more.

I didn't absorb the weight of that moment at the time. I was enjoying the chance to be a proud uncle. Brandt's brother Haymes, my oldest nephew, wore the white caddy coveralls and carried his brother's clubs. It thrilled me to watch both of them on Augusta National. Especially when Brandt birdied "Amen Corner," the course's treacherous 11th, 12th, and 13th holes that leave the best golfers praying to the golf gods.

Brandt's career was on the upswing. My career was going in a different direction. I went from being *the* guy at Allegiant to *a* guy at National City. With the deal complete, I transitioned to become National City's president and chief executive of Missouri banking.

The newness of being a part of this massive company was exciting at the start. I went to Cleveland and made a presentation via teleconference about the St. Louis market, and in short order, I joined National City's executive development program, or EDP. The program involved trips, conference calls, and work culminating in a presentation to the senior executives. Your project either had to raise revenue or lower cost.

The people in the program were brilliant. My group included a man in his early 30s who graduated top of his class at Harvard Law and went to work for the consulting firm McKinsey & Company before coming to National City. He was a rising star in retail banking and unbelievable to work with. He also cared about my thoughts and ideas, partly because they were solid, but partly due to the company's caring, engaging culture.

The company was full of people like that. I always enjoyed surrounding myself with smart people. But even with all of these great minds, everything in National City was siloed. I was stuck in my narrow spot and didn't see a point in worrying about the bigger picture. There was no incentive to take big risks or think outside of the box.

My new role allowed me to redouble my efforts as a husband and father. I took my son Stephen to Europe for a father-son trip, and Kelly and I took Brooks and Ryan to Africa for the trip of a lifetime. For the first time in my professional career, I could step away from work without worrying about the day-to-day operations. I would simply check in here and there when I was on vacation, and that was that.

My job provided my family with some unbelievable experiences. I was tasked with overseeing National City's charity spending in St. Louis, which allowed my kids insider access pretty much anywhere they went. The neatest was the St. Louis Zoo, which is one of the top zoos in the country.

The female tiger at the zoo had babies, and I got a call. "Do you want to come down and see them?" Yes! Kelly and I took Paige, Jack, Brooks, and Ryan, and they got to pet a baby tiger. We were in the cages underneath the zoo's tiger area with a black panther about 20 feet from us. That panther kept its eye on Jack.

"Jack, the panther is thinking you'd make a good snack," the handler told him. Another time, the Hayes family got a private seal show. Ryan got to hold a fish in his hand that the seal jumped up and grabbed from him.

Through all of my charity and board connections, I was shifting from a godfather in banking to a community leader. I was involved in cool decisions that made St. Louis a better place and impacted people's lives. And I got a crash course in politics, committees, and how decisions get made.

I sat on the board of St. Louis University, and Father Lawrence Biondi, the longtime president, wanted to build a 10,000-seat arena that became the Chaifetz Arena. He outlined a plan to raise nearly $80 million in outside capital, and we approved the measure. We signed off on decisions for building dorms and adding programming. Other boards I served on included Wyman Center, Forest Park Forever, St. Louis Sports Commission, and Purcell Tire & Rubber Co.

Groups looked to me for my business acumen. I spoke to the Association for Corporate Growth St. Louis to discuss how good, timely decisions can pay off in a big way—which is a curious topic, given what would happen in the years ahead.

The media burnished my reputation further. *The Post-Dispatch* wrote a profile of me in 2005. "Shaun Hayes cuts quite a figure: a banking executive with an Ozark accent and blond hair that is borderline shaggy. He can be disarmingly casual, like a surfer dude stuffed into a navy-blue business suit."

Though I presented this image of success and enjoyment, I put on this false face of a disarmingly casual banking executive as an inner struggle brewed.

The board commitments were meaningful, but they couldn't account for everything I had lost in transitioning from Allegiant to National City. I didn't need to devote much mental capacity to my job since there weren't challenges and problems to solve. National City didn't need me for my banking experience. I was there to put a familiar face on this operation so National City wouldn't appear like an outsider in St. Louis. My job was to shake hands, give sound bites, and be a booster for National City. They even had me talking to bankers from places like Florida and California on behalf of the company as they tried to do larger, more meaningful acquisitions in higher growth markets.

Money and attention can only take you so far when you're not doing what you love.

Looking back, I don't regret selling Allegiant. Our bank had run its course, and we sold it for a lot of money to a large and storied institution. But I was a fish out of water on the corporate side. It just wasn't me. As an entrepreneur told me years later, "You should have just left banking and set up a private investment firm." *Yeah, probably.* That would have nourished my soul.

But that's not the road I took. I followed an easy and comfortable path, and by the time I realized how far away from my goals I'd drifted, a piece of myself was gone. As the honeymoon phase wore off with National City, my job made me feel dead inside. I went from getting my high of making daily deals to becoming some listless guy with an empty title.

I had a position, and I was making good money. A lot of my money was tied up in National City stock, which gave me an incentive to follow this path and play out the string. But with contentment so elusive, I began pursuing more outside investments and real estate deals. I owned six Lion's Choice roast beef fast food restaurant franchises, and my friend and I owned three plastic companies. At one point I had 71 LLCs to my name.

I was on the board of directors for Isle of Capri Casinos, which was a fun and satisfying opportunity. The company operated riverboat and dockside casinos across seven states. There was so much vetting in the casino business. States don't simply hand out gaming licenses. It was harder, in fact, to get casino approval than bank approval from the Federal Reserve.

They looked at *everything*. Every check, every loan, every business decision. The investigators went door to door at one point talking to our neighbors. They didn't find anything that raised red flags. Sure, I was aggressive. Sure, I operated in the gray. But as far as the government was concerned, after a quarter century in banking, I was clean. Leaning on sound legal and accounting advice throughout my career had kept me from slipping.

Another venture that spoke to my stellar reputation was a possibility suggested by my friend, Art Weiss: becoming the owner of the NHL's St. Louis Blues. Bill Laurie and Nancy Walton Laurie were looking to sell the team—the husband and wife bought the Blues in 1999—but it seemed like their heart was never really in it.

But hockey?

If I could own any sports team, it would be the St. Louis Cardinals. Unfortunately, the timing wasn't right. The team was sold in 1995 to a group that included Bill DeWitt Jr., whose father had owned teams, too. The Cardinals have been owned by the same group now for a quarter century.

While running the Cardinals was not an option, the NHL's St. Louis Blues represented an entry into the upper crust. Lots of people in the United States have money. But there are only 124 teams in the four major North American pro sports leagues. Being able to own a team in a sports city like St. Louis only sweetened the deal.

Not bad for a kid from Thayer!

My banking background gave me a leg up in the pro sports industry. Allegiant flipped and sold historic tax credit for the Cardinals' Busch Stadium in 2003, and Allegiant was also the official bank of the NFL's Rams. There was also my experience on the St. Louis Sports Commission.

But owning a team was something else entirely.

"I think we can do this with you as the front guy," Art told me. "You're credible, willing to put some money in it, and people will follow you."

I didn't know anything about running a hockey team, but I had some ideas and knew how to raise money. We developed a business plan. Local business leaders pledged one to five million. Three different groups emerged as favorites to become the next owner of the team and arena. One was headed by me. Another, a private equity group called Sports Capital Partners, was led by businessman and basketball executive Dave Checketts.

Our bid came in at $103 million. Checketts' group bid $125 million, and the other St. Louis group bid something like $105 million.

Checketts' group had the inside track and an exclusive negotiating window. It looked like it was all over. We had some fun imagining what it'd be like to run a sports team, but it was time to move on with our lives.

Following those stalled negotiations, it seemed that we had another chance at owning the Blues. I was on a Christmas shopping trip in New York with my wife when my phone started blowing up with calls and texts.

I spent hours on the phone talking to our investors and came back with a second bid before Checketts' group finally locked down the deal. When all was said and done, Sports Capital Partners ended up losing investors tens of millions of dollars over the course of owning the team—but none of it was Checketts' money. It was a lesson I've learned and relearned so many times. Smart investing means diminishing your personal risk. I should have kept that in mind myself.

Sometimes the best deals are the ones you don't make.

As we were jockeying to buy the Blues, I was working on another smaller deal—this one with my nephew, Haymes. It was also 2005, the year Hurricane Katrina slammed the gulf coast and another storm, Hurricane Dennis, passed the city of Gulf Shores where Haymes and his wife live. The Alabama coastline is beautiful—mile after mile of white sand beaches. The location stood out to me, and as the region rebuilt, I saw huge growth opportunity.

My nephew and his law partner were doing small real estate deals, and I spoke about the opportunity to my real estate partners in St. Louis. We found the perfect location to build either a hotel or condo property.

I didn't know much about beach property development. But since we had a good plan and the right location, I didn't ask many questions. I also didn't listen to my instincts, and looking back,

I wish I had. As it was with a lot of my investments during that 2005 to 2007 time period, I was a little too trusting. For so long, banking and real estate were sure, safe bets for me, and I took that success for granted.

It was all easy, and I simply went along with things.

In short order, all hell would break loose.

CHAPTER 9
FIREWORKS

Growing up, I worked at a motel. I rented rooms and interact-ed with adults as a child frequently, which gave me the ability to read and understand people. I developed a street intelligence that most people never obtain.

That background fueled my early interest in business. Dating back to the jobs and money-making schemes I pursued in my teens and early 20s, I was always trying to game the system.

From ages 16 to 19, I worked as a laborer baling hay. After cutting the grass, I'd use a mower conditioner to treat it, then rake and bale it. I got 25 cents to haul it and a dollar for each bale. My friend's father had a truck that we were able to use to haul every-thing, so we had no equipment costs.

After a while, I moved from baling to driving the truck. I hired two or three guys and paid them. I used a portion of the earnings to pay for gas and any other overhead and pocketed the rest of the profits. We would work from 10 a.m. until dark, drank all night, and started over again the next day. We made a killing.

By 1980, macroeconomic trends brought an end to our hay baling days. That summer, President Jimmy Carter had an agricultural embargo with Russia. Agriculture *died*, baling twine cost a fortune, and the price of oil and gas doubled. I wound up working at my cousin's wife's gift shop, and between gas and lunch, I wasn't making any money. But I got to look at a lot of cute women.

"You need a real job," my dad told me.

He had a point. But what could I do? It got me thinking about Thayer. Every Fourth of July, my hometown hosted a full slate of baseball games, from the seven-year-olds to fifteen-year-olds, and after the last game finished there was a huge fireworks display run by the volunteer fire department. I called Mr. Dawe who oversaw the fireworks show.

"Mr. Dawe, where do you get the fireworks?"

"I get them at Arnold Fireworks in North Little Rock, Arkansas."

I went home and dialed information. This was long before Google. I was connected with Arnold Fireworks, who I learned was a wholesaler.

"Can I speak to the owner?"

"I'm the owner, Margaret Arnold," the woman on the line responded. "My husband died a couple of years ago."

"How do I get fireworks? And by the way, I don't have any money."

"I can give them to you on consignment," she told me. "There's just one problem. It's past the first of June. You have to have your order in by then because we send a truck up your way. You'd have to pick up the fireworks yourself."

"No problem. My family's got plenty of trucks."

I drove to Arkansas a few days later, loaded up the fireworks on the back of a pickup, and made the return trip. It rained all the way back.

I drove 150 miles with a truck bed full of fireworks. You couldn't sell fireworks in Thayer, but past the city limits on the north end of town, there was a bar called the Blue Moon and my dad owned the real estate. It was a suitable base of operations. My dad and I built a fireworks stand. It wasn't pretty, but it got the job done. I painted "Discount Fireworks" on the back, and I got two four-by-eight pieces of plywood and went to the neighbors on the south and north sides of the highway.

"Can I put my sign up on your fence?" I asked.

"Of course," they said.

There was a mimeograph machine at the school. My friend's mom was a secretary, and she let me make copies using green paper: "Bottle rockets 99 cents gross, discount fireworks, one mile north of city limits, Highway 63, Thayer, Missouri." I went to all the grocery stores that Saturday and stuck the sheets under the windshield wipers of the cars parked in the parking lots.

I was officially in the fireworks business.

I also took advantage of any opportunities that came up. If a kid pulled up in a Lincoln or Cadillac and their parents gave them a $50 or $100 bill, guess how much fireworks they bought? Fifty or 100. *Oh, it's $47.25 plus tax.*

Early on, even with the bar right next door, the drunks weren't even buying from me. But when the first of July came around, I started selling fireworks like crazy at margins of 400%. During his trips to and from the St. Louis racetracks, I also had my dad pick up fireworks along the way so we would turn around and sell them at markup. One buyer had a farm about a mile up the road.

"What's this three-inch shell?" he asked.

"Oh, it's a wonderful thing," I said. I didn't know. I wasn't an expert on this stuff. Two days later, he came back.

"If you weren't so big, I would kick your ass," he said.

"Whatya mean?"

"My kids and I set off those fireworks the other night. And the last one was the three-inch shell. You're right. It was beautiful. But it's a mortar round. I ended up chasing cattle until two in the morning."

I made $20,000 for three weeks of work, which was a lot of money back then. The next summer, I didn't have to worry about getting a job because I ordered my fireworks in May from Mrs. Arnold and had them shipped. I was in business. During the following summers, even into my time at UMB, my cousin took over the operation. I would chip in, and we would split the money.

Fireworks gave way during my junior year of college to a more dangerous and explosive opportunity as a loan shark, which I didn't realize at the time was illegal. I didn't know any better. I just thought I was taking advantage of a need. Rich students were bound to get money from their parents each week—but sometimes they needed money *now* for a football game or a hot date.

"Shaun, my parents are going to put $500 in my account on Monday," they'd say. "I need a couple hundred bucks."

"No problem. You write me a check for $220, and I'll give you a check for $200." I would have them go and cash the check from me. Meanwhile, I would mail their checks to my bank. I banked in Arkansas, so it would take a few days to get the money added back.

I started making these loans, and to get money flowing, I had a girl at a sorority house and a guy at a frat house each give me a few thousand dollars so I had more capital to lend. I charged 10% a week. I gave them a few hundred dollars a month and they were making money on money.

I also took out a student loan for $1,500 at 4% interest. So, I had my cash, the student loan, the sorority girl's and fraternity guy's money in the pot, and that gave me more money to lend with.

One of my frat brothers had a friend who had a bookie in St. Charles, and I helped to coordinate bets. With betting, you'd place $100 on a college game, and if you lost, you'd bet $200 on another game. Then if you lost again, you'd bet $400 on a pro game. If you lost again, you bet $800 on a three o'clock game, and if you lost again you bet $1,600 on the Monday night game. If you lost, you owed four or five grand to the bookie, then you'd come to me, and I'd write you a check.

These students didn't recognize the randomness of outcomes, and they were losing lots of money, which meant lots of transactions. I was doing all this lending, and guys were losing money gambling, and that was the jet fuel on the fire.

I went home for Thanksgiving and the bank called me.

"We know you're kiting checks," they told me. "It has to stop." I was running tens of thousands of dollars each week.

I couldn't talk to my parents about it. But I did call a cousin who's 10 years older and asked if his dad would call the bank on my behalf to ensure that I was in the clear. I didn't need the bank on my bad side.

One kid who owed money to the bookie reached out to me. "I need to meet you," he said. I met with him at a truck stop 35 miles away. It was dark and cold, and he had his dad and brothers there, and they were threatening to kill me. "You can beat me—there's three of you. But did you ask your son how he got here?"

"No."

"I sent him to the bookie I know. What would happen if he didn't pay?"

"Well, they would break a bone."

"A bone?"

"Yeah." The dad paid me with no juice.

Between my fear of getting crushed by the bank or someone who was out a lot of money, I was finished as a loan shark.

Those early business endeavors, for better or worse, provided a foundation for my professional career. They showed me how to take risks and gave me confidence in my ability to work through problems. I could maneuver my way out of anything. Or so I thought.

CHAPTER 10
ARMAGEDDON

The storm was unrelenting. There was an F5 tornado that lev-eled and smashed everything in its path. A lot of people in banking and real estate—including me—couldn't recognize the storm approaching until it was too late.

The global financial crisis that began in 2007 was a once-in-a-lifetime storm and the most disruptive force in banking and economics since the Great Depression.

Many of the problems centered around risk. People wanted to live the dream and own their own homes. With low interest rates, they felt confident relying on credit—including subprime or high-risk lending—to make their dreams come true. Financial institutions were more than happy to extend those lines of credit, knowing they could repossess and resell the property if the borrower defaulted.

That system could be lucrative in a strong housing market. But in 2006 and 2007, the housing market softened. Borrowers struggled to refinance and didn't have the resources to pay off their loans. The lenders were stuck with a bunch of repossessed houses that they struggled to sell. It was the scenario I had feared years earlier at Allegiant when we gave away Edge Mortgage.

As it turned out, a lot of financial institutions were living on the edge.

One of those institutions was National City, which prided itself on being *so smart*. They were always educating employees, and their risk-management leader came across as hyper-intellectual. He was one of the most pompous people I've met in banking, and that's saying something when you consider it's a profession filled with pompous people.

Turns out, they weren't as smart as they thought they were.

National City often highlighted the money made in mortgage lending, but *they didn't say they were sitting on billions of dollars in subprime loans.* In fact, they were one of the country's largest subprime lenders. Their mortgage operation was built on a house of cards. Maybe I didn't ask the right questions or wasn't paying enough attention. I just didn't realize the level of risk that National City was taking on.

Being coddled, insulated, and siloed, I wasn't able to recognize the problems that caused National City's undoing or the macro trends that upended the financial world.

I began to glimpse the truth in 2007, as National City's stock began its freefall. That summer in Cleveland after a president's meeting, a few of us talked, and we couldn't understand the huge mortgage exposure. National City's leadership was so hung up on credit default swaps that they weren't looking at the underlying asset. They weren't thinking about the people living in the house and paying the mortgage. The realization was another signal that corporate banking wasn't for me. I missed making deals and having an impact.

I'd wound up in the type of career I'd wanted to avoid—a boring, dissatisfying existence adrift in a giant sea. I yearned for the energy of my Allegiant days.

Even with the economy struggling, I found myself wanting to recreate the world I lost. Call it overconfidence or foolishness, but I believed I could succeed where other banks like National City stumbled.

I envisioned running a bank through a franchise model. My team would come up with 75% of the money, and a local banker running the day-to-day operations would come up with the other 25% and develop a local board. I could build a network of these community banks south of I-70 and east of I-55 that would cover the Southeast and Midwest in states like Alabama, Mississippi, Florida, Georgia, and Tennessee.

We could set up in decent-sized towns. A network of ten $100 million banks would make us a billion-dollar bank, and I would come up with the bulk of the capital. I had the connections, and the banks would have a local presence. With centralized operations, we could do economies of scale.

These were a few opportunities that emerged that would have

been steady and stable, including running UMB's St. Louis operations. But I wanted something I could have fun with.

I ended up calling an old friend named Louis Ahlmeyer, whom I had known since 1984 when I came to St. Louis with UMB. Louis was the leading shareholder of Investors Financial Corporation of Pettis County, Inc., (IFC), a holding company for Excel Bank based in Sedalia with a population of 20,000 in central Missouri.

Excel was the sort of community bank that I knew, and it would be a challenge and a chance to generate some income. It was about a $200 million bank at the time.

I convinced Louis to sell me his shares and ended up owning 54% of the stock. Along with the law firm Thompson Coburn, Don Hutson—head of the banking department for the accounting and advisory firm BKD—handled all of the paperwork for regulatory approval. I figured I could send loans to Excel that National City wouldn't do. Excel was an investment to me, not a place to land.

As the leading shareholder, director, and vice chairman, I carried influence. I guided the opening of a loan production office and hired Tim Murphy, a banking buddy, as the primary loan officer. With Tim in that role, I could steer commercial real estate loans to Excel and get them approved.

My other investments at the time were seeing mixed results. I saw potential in the land I owned with Michael Litz, the longtime friend and real estate developer, through McKnight Man LLC. We signed a deal with Target in 2007 to put a store on that corner of McKnight and Manchester in Rock Hill.

At the same time, my land investment in Alabama was going sideways. I took a trip with my boys Brooks and Ryan to visit the property and see my nephew Haymes. What the investors didn't mention until many years later was that they had an offer to walk away with $5 million, but they thought we could make $10 million apiece if we held out longer. We couldn't, of course.

The storm clouds became more obvious—and ominous—by early 2008. Especially where National City was concerned. Dividends were slashed, jobs were cut, and departments shuttered. Shares tumbled. This unsinkable bank was taking on water, which was a problem for me since my Allegiant money was tied up in National City stock.

At the same time, I was going underwater. In April 2008, *St. Louis Small Business Monthly* named me one of the 12 top St. Louis entrepreneurs in the past 20 years. It was a huge honor. But at the time I was named to that list, I didn't feel like a great entrepreneur at all. I was spiraling and looking for a place to land.

Don Hutson alerted me to an opportunity with Sun Security Bank, a $365 million bank scattered from St. Charles to Springfield and the Lake of the Ozarks. The bank was owned by Elmer Austermann, a man in his upper 70s who ruled with an iron fist. He focused on every nickel—and I mean every little nickel—that was spent. There was no outside cleaning crew. Bank employees emptied trash cans and cleaned restrooms.

Tom Daiber and I had talked to Elmer in 2002 about buying the bank when we were looking for Allegiant acquisitions, but nothing ever materialized. The bank was in disarray by the time I took a second look at it. The government wanted a management change and capital infusion—my specialties. It seemed like a good fit. I left National City and joined Sun Security as a partner and president on August 1, 2008. A few months later, PNC scooped up National City at a discount of about five billion dollars. One hundred and sixty-three years of legacy banking washed away. At the time of the sale, National City's stock price had tumbled all the way to $2.07. It was selling at about $33 when we reached the Allegiant deal. This meant that my National City stock, once worth $14 million, had lost more than 90% of its value.

National City's failings motivated me. I went into Sun Security with a plan. But Elmer and I were totally night and day. He fought back at every turn about every suggestion. Even so, I was back in charge again. My first order of business was to put the band back together. I wanted to take the people and elements that had worked so well at Allegiant and apply them to this new venture. I got my risk-management guy and a young credit guy to come over, and we started cleaning up the place. I had all the branch presidents meet for dinner in Rolla. They were located in 17 little towns and had never met each other.

But even with some familiar faces, everything felt different, like we were trying to paddle upstream. The banking world wasn't the same one I had worked in years earlier.

I didn't think things could get lower. But with the economy

in tatters, things kept going lower and lower. The bank regulators were behind every curve, rooting through past issues and looking harder and harder at everything.

We were making some good loans that were generating cash-flow, but not enough of them. Banks weren't lending, and people still needed to borrow money.

As I was trying to straighten out Sun Security, Richard Miller, another longtime banking contact, cornered me and asked me to invest a million dollars into Truman Bank, which had four branches scattered across St. Louis.

"Don't worry. St. Louis Bank will lend you the money," said Richard, a tough negotiator who, years before, had milked an extra $200,000 out of selling his Kansas City religious radio station to Jimmy Swaggart's group in a cash deal.

He got me to commit, too, and I was brought on with Truman as a consultant.

I didn't do enough due diligence with any of these opportunities. Notice a pattern? I was overconfident and desperate—the gambler who hit it big and keeps playing as their chip count dwindles. Like the other two banks, Truman was buried in bad loans related to raw land and new construction. Excel was in the best shape of the three and qualified for four million dollars in Troubled Assets Relief Program (TARP) money in 2009. But even with the federal funding, the bank was in a precarious position. I wasn't ready to admit that I was in over my head, growing more and more desperate as the banks floundered. Things were so much different than they were during my Allegiant years, and I just wasn't ready to face that reality.

I aimed to prop up Truman, save Sun, keep building Excel, and do things the right way. I wanted to save the day and be the hero.

And then I was faced with a scenario that put me on my road to ruin.

For 15 years, I had people bring me deals. I would go to another bank to arrange the financing based on whatever collateral I needed to put up along with my personal guarantee. This strategy had made me millions of dollars.

In 2009, my sometime business partner Mike Litz (the brilliant guy who invited a horse to his indoor wedding) and people in his office brought me a deal on some apartments they owned in North St. Louis County. I'd done these kinds of deals many times. Bank of America was owed $3.7 million for the 128-apartment complex, and they had a note tied up for $900,000. Michael and his partners wanted to refinance. Additional collateral would give them fix-up money in working capital. This was a good loan, but it had to be completed before the end of March to keep Bank of America happy.

I saw a win-win scenario for everyone, and I made a fateful decision. I had Excel review and underwrite the loan, and I was going to be a benefactor—meaning I stood to make $300,000 on the loan to keep me going for a few months. I shouldn't have participated in the deal. Since I benefited from the proceeds, it was technically illegal.

But it was a slam dunk. A sure thing.

I made another mistake in a separate deal involving Mike months later. I saw an opportunity that I'd learned about 20 years earlier on financing discounted debt using credit-worthy borrowers. Mike owed about $15 million at National City and Centrue, and we could buy the debt for $8 million and add a $1 million fee for the bank. Mike would not be the borrower, but he had three good, solid borrowers who could each independently cover their three million dollars. All Mike had to do was honor his agreement to manage, fix, and sell houses. His company and the borrower would split the net profit.

But once the deal closed, Mike Litz didn't do anything. He'd set the investors and the banks up to fail. I couldn't believe he would do this to all of us. He let everything fall apart.

Those nine million dollars in loans at Excel became the final nail in my personal coffin.

The transaction closed in August 2009, and Centrue, at the last minute, made us buy a loan in which I was a guarantor on the package. I didn't want to be sued, so I agreed. If the transaction had gone as planned, it would have never been an issue—but it didn't. Nothing went according to plan.

The problems I faced because of Mike paled in comparison to the havoc he caused for many prospective homeowners. Through his companies, he sold wraparound mortgages, which are a second form of mortgage on top of the payments for the first mortgage. In many cases, he failed to make the payments to the original mortgage holder, leaving many would-be homeowners booted from their dream homes. It was tragic.

The full scope of the damage would take years to unravel.

My own bad fortunes extended to my investments in Alabama. After LaSalle bank sold to Bank of America, BOA decided to collect on the unpaid loans. Raw ground was not a hot or safe investment, even if it was at the corner of 98 and 59—the main corner of Gulf Shores, Alabama. We fought to drag things out. When it went to court, we had nothing to stand on.

The judgment came down, and it was crushing. A summary judgment for $10.2 million. It was a heavy toll, and no one wanted to lend to me anymore.

The poor outcomes and poor decisions represented the dangers of living in the gray areas. I could have been fine if this had happened, or *if* that person would have held up their agreement, or *if* the transactions would have gone through the proper channels.

There were too many *ifs* and too much left to chance. Instead of worrying about right and wrong—and I certainly knew which was which—I focused on survival and getting myself out of a jam.

Just enough gray had clouded my entire thinking. I tried to wish it all away or move on.

But I couldn't. I was a dead man walking with connections to three doomed banks.

CHAPTER 11
DRIP, DRIP, DRIP

The waiting was hell.

I was waiting for everything to fall apart. Waiting for the government to build a case. Waiting to hit rock bottom.

When you commit a typical crime, the investigation starts immediately. But with bank crimes and bank regulators, it can take years for the government to even recognize that a crime had been committed. The wheels of justice are as fast as a leaky faucet: *drip, drip, drip.*

My downfall, in essence, came down to time and money. I didn't have the money to fix the messes I'd created. So now it was just a matter of time, and time was fluid. It stood still and raced forward and flew backward—all at once.

I stopped paying my mortgage in 2011. I couldn't afford it anymore. There was something so royally demoralizing about going from a banking power broker to flat broke. I couldn't pay loans. I sold most of my assets and my home was in foreclosure.

As my life was crashing around me, my banking career was ending. Elmer Austermann, Sun Security Bank's combative chief executive, invited me to a meeting at Panera Bread.

"This isn't going to work," he said of my working at Sun Security Bank, and I agreed. Our personalities clashed, and the hole I was trying to dig us out of was a lot bigger than I initially realized. Pretty soon, all three banks I was associated with—Excel, Sun Security, and Truman—would fail. The government was finally closing banks rather than letting them die a slow death.

Excel's death was the most dramatic. The FDIC downgraded it in 2009 from a "2" risk-management composite to a "4," which represents a deficient asset quality. The FDIC cited the growth of the loan portfolio as a main driver of the problem, but in reality, some of those seeds of collapse were already present before I entered the mix. By 2010, the bank's risk was downgraded again to a "5," or "critically deficient," putting the bank's future in doubt.

The regulators noted my problem loans with Michael Litz.

"Mr. Hayes is personally involved in business ventures with Michael Litz, who is one of the owners of Eighteen Investments, Inc. This is of concern because it appears that Mr. Hayes was instrumental in bringing this concentration to Excel Bank through his business relationships," the FDIC wrote.

On October 19, 2012, the Missouri Division of Finance closed Excel Bank. Simmons First National Bank purchased Excel's assets and took on its deposits.

Truman Bank faced the same fate.

After my rise at UMB, our growth years at Allegiant, and orchestrating the sale of a $2.5-billion bank, my banking career was finished. While it was tough to see the banks closed and sad to realize the impact those closures had on employees and the greater community, it was a relief for me to be out of the banking business. Banking wasn't the same anymore.

For the first time in my life, I was unemployed. I had so many problems financially, I didn't know what to do first. My reputation was in tatters. I was dubbed a "banking bad boy" in newspaper headlines. I was battling with Midwest Regional Bank in court. St. Louis Bank sued me, too, over defaulted loans.

I was selling anything I could to pay people in order to placate them. I paid back tens of millions of dollars of debt, but no one remembers that—they remember who didn't get paid. I'll drive down streets of St. Louis now and think about the buildings. *I used to own that.* I unloaded my interest in so many properties and investments to pay people. Some of my LLCs filed for Chapter 11 bankruptcy protection, including one that involved my Lion's Choice franchise restaurants. My empire was cratering. My marriage was, too. I shielded my wife from as many of my issues as I could since she knew next to nothing about my business dealings. But there would be a point where I couldn't sugarcoat or downplay the issues anymore.

I spent my whole life thinking I was in control. But I wasn't in control of anything anymore. All I really had control over was the type of alcohol in my glass. I shifted from cabernet to vodka because it was cheap and easy, and it *burned*. I drank six out of seven nights a week. Alcohol helped me forget what I'd lost or was in the process of losing.

I needed to forget—to wash it all away.

It reminded me how out of control I felt when my sons Brooks and Ryan were in California waiting for school to start, and Brooks had a brain aneurysm. We were on the phone, trying to gather details, and my chest was a jackhammer. I called a friend of mine who's an anesthesiologist, and he took me to the hospital to treat my panic attack. The stress tore me apart inside.

The next morning, my secretary got me the first flight out. The line at security was 300 people deep. I wasn't going to make it out. I went to the front line and lost it. The dam burst. Sobbing. Tears. "My son's having surgery." I was able to get on the flight and be there for Brooks. He was in intensive care for 10 days. Thankfully, he was able to make a full recovery.

A few months later, I went in for a physical. I was used to running every day, but I was just exhausted. "Shaun, you're getting old," my doctor told me. Something wasn't right, so they ran some tests. I was at Busch Stadium a few days later walking into the last businessperson's special of the Cardinals' season when my doctor called me back.

"You're missing three pints of blood," he told me. "Something is really wrong. I want you here in the morning."

They tested me for everything. Was it a disease? Something I picked up on a previous vacation?

The only thing they noticed was that my spleen was severely enlarged. I went in for surgery to have it removed. The surgeon came by.

"Your spleen was the size of the football, and it should be the size of your fist. We almost had to cut you open. It was the biggest thing I've ever taken out arthroscopically," he said.

An oncologist broke the news: it was cancer.

"Don't tell me any more. Let me call my wife. Can you come back when she's here?" I asked. I knew whatever he told me, I wouldn't repeat to her correctly. She has that lawyer mindset. They sent me to a top-flight physician named Nancy Bartlett at the Siteman Cancer Center.

I got a CT scan. I was worried. What if this was it? Anytime that "c" word gets tossed around, you start to consider odds and stages, *life expectancy.*

The results came in. No more cancer. It was all confined to my spleen.

A clean bill of health.

I'd been given another chance to make things right.

But being cancer-free didn't resolve my financial issues. My father's words from years earlier kept bouncing around in my head. "It's all about cashflow." Without being able to get credit, I struggled putting opportunities together. But I knew people. And I had ideas. I kicked around the possibility of owning radio stations, properties, or maybe something else. Maybe I could get back into the fireworks business!

Old investment or business partners would come out of the woodwork in search of opportunities. One of those people was Christine Zerjav, whom I hadn't talked to since my Allegiant days 14 years prior.

"Shaun, let's look at the adult daycare business," she suggested. The care and companionship option are for seniors who still live at home. The math was intriguing, especially with more and more people reaching retirement age and the opportunity for Medicaid funds.

I negotiated deals with the landlord of an apartment building that the Catholic Church had built around 1970. We took the common area, since it featured a community room, and put an adult daycare in it. Cambridge Adult Day Care. One of the investors was an accountant. Little by little, we started to see income trickling in—four to eight grand a month. I saw a business.

Charles Lehnbeuter (a longtime business contact) and I bought the building.

Chris Jansen also came out of the woodwork during this tough time.

Chris had a company that made cabinets, and he figured out the real niche was doing cabinet installs for Verizon and other corporate customers. They did a turnkey operation, and he made a ton of money and ended up buying a marina, a jet, and all of the trappings of excess.

He latched onto me in early 2012, right around the time I was having my surgery. I hadn't seen the guy in 12 or 13 years.

I had office space in Clayton, and he and his sons ended up sharing the space, so we did some deals together.

He used my connections to set meetings and try to get fees out of these people. This raised red flags for me because everything was transactional for him.

We had bought some debt from banks for a women's spa, and I set up a deal. He tried to take over and run it. The partner was a woman I brought to the table, and she threw him out. He thought I had a deal with her even though I didn't. He and his boys thought they were private detectives.

Of all the problems that came my way, many of them had some connection with Chris. He had goaded someone, given someone bad intel, or tried to bring me down in some way. When you start a business, it's like being on Lake Michigan on January 1 in a speedo for a polar bear plunge. You jump in that water, and the first thing you're thinking about is grabbing anyone's hand you can. And that hand feels so comforting and warm.

But those warm sentiments cooled pretty quickly. That's how

it went with Chris, and it got to the point where his sons were following me around, tailing me as I walked through the city. Trust me, *I'm not that interesting.*

One day in 2013, I got a call from my wife, Kelly. I immediately knew something was wrong. "A creditor is here, and they're taking our furniture and my coat and my jewelry and our silver," she told me. I later found it was a tip from Chris.

I learned that the FBI was looking into me. I met with them for a couple hours a few weeks later. Every day could be the day it all came crashing down.

Drip.

I stayed in constant contact with my attorney. Because the U.S. Attorney's Office was so leaky, he had a source through which he got consistent updates.

"They passed on you," he told me.

Thank God. I was in the clear. For now.

While the FBI was off my tail, the government wasn't done with me. In late 2013, the FDIC, or Federal Deposit Insurance Corporation, permanently barred me from banking. Their order stated that I "engaged or participated in violations of law or regulation, unsafe or unsound practices, and/or breaches of fiduciary duty as an institution-affiliated party" of Excel Bank. And that my conduct at Excel "involved personal dishonesty" and the willful "disregard for the safety or soundness of the bank."

It stung to see those words in writing. I know in my heart that that wasn't my intent. But my wishes didn't change the fact that I had made some major missteps. It was an end to a great career. But again, *there was nothing I could do to fix the problems.* I felt like a defenseless punching bag. All I could do was duck my head, take the hit, and try to erase it all from my mind and move forward.

But the hits kept coming. I got a call from Ladue police saying there was a warrant for my arrest for lack of payment for child support. My first wife Sandra needed $100,000 for tuition, but bills were piling up. The first night, I slept in my office. Then I moved to a franchise adult daycare center in St. Charles for a few weeks. I laid low and tried to stay off the grid. But then a contact from my banking days saw me at Panera Bread and gladly turned me in to police.

Drip.

I spent seven days in jail. Two different friends came up with $25,000 each to cover my release. The time in custody was odd—demoralizing and embarrassing. Upon my release, I was put on a strict payment plan. The walls continued to close in, and in my mind, everything tied back to my stumbles and missteps. My mistakes. The newspapers got clever with their adjectives in describing me. *Contentious. Beleaguered.* They might as well have called me a no-good, two-timing bastard.

Even so, I remained hopeful that my worst days were behind me.

I remained hopeful about this adult daycare plan. Through

a franchising model, we charged $30,000 and got some investors with us in 2014 and 2015. We sold franchises across the St. Louis area—St. Charles, Branson, Springfield, Dexter. We were even looking out of state in Memphis, Tennessee.

But after eight months of time, travel, and optimism about Memphis, we got news that there wasn't any interest in the bond offering. We had a conference call, and I raised the same points I had eight months earlier: *Shouldn't this be a startup?* It has no collateral, and the cash flow has to build over time, and you only have the bond proceeds reserves. Of course, everyone had the most southern way of making you feel good even when things were bad, but I didn't feel good at all. A closure was coming by the end of the year on the apartment building in Memphis because of the stupid move to bring on a receiver for investor benefit. While this offered tremendous upside and capital gains, now everything was going down.

It seemed like nothing could go right for very long. A state examiner for senior services started poking around our business, throwing around misappropriation accusations that were unfounded. *The St. Louis Business Journal* reached out about writing an article about me.

My attorney and I talked about participating in the story. *Why not?* We expected a positive article about Cambridge. Instead, it was a negative.

"A person involved in a real estate transaction to purchase the property that houses the first Cambridge Adult Day Care told *The Business Journal* that federal authorities are investigating the deal.

The Business Journal also found that parts of the day care business were registered to a UPS Store box, which is impermissible, according to the Missouri Secretary of State's Office, and that a person soliciting investments on Cambridge's behalf from California may be doing so without a license required by that state."[2]

The article relied on quotes from investor Ray Bax, who claimed that I had promised to get a federal Housing and Urban Development loan to replace a loan he had received and how he would get a "guarantor's fee." I did not promise him that. Bax later got the business put into receivership and contacted the FBI. They looked at it up and down and found nothing criminal. All of Bax's talking points seemed to come from Chris Jansen.

The centers were struggling. Some of them closed. I wanted to scale up but didn't want to be in a business I couldn't scale, and Christine and Charles wanted no interest in the franchise operation.

The centers closing were my last gasps. I didn't have any business prospects on the horizon. In December 2015, I was in a lawyer's office. I couldn't afford him at that point, but while I was there, he called the U.S. attorney's office to check on the status of the swirling investigations with me listening.

"Are you going to indict him?"

"Yes, any day."

---

2   Kirn, Jacob. "Shaun Hayes' new venture." St. Louis Business Journal, March 20, 2015, https://www.bizjournals.com/stlouis/print-edition/2015/03/20/shaun-hayes-new-venture.html.

That was a week before Christmas.

Drip.

My family was going to be homeless, and my marriage was finished. Kelly and I began packing and throwing stuff away. Our next-door neighbors made a generous offer to Kelly. "We know you're getting foreclosed on. We spend the winters in Florida. Use our house." Their master suite was on one end, and we lived on the other end of the house. We stayed there from January to March, at which point Kelly found a place for her and the kids to live. I wasn't welcome, and so I was more or less homeless. I slept in my car. Sometimes I stayed at one of our daycare centers. I would arrive after it closed for the night and would wake up and shower and leave before it opened for the morning.

I had failed everyone—most of all my children.

There was no more hustling.

No more running.

The first week of January 2016 was the closest I came to thinking about ending it all. Killing myself would bring an end to all this suffering.

The sad part was that I didn't have a $10 million life insurance policy anymore. My life wasn't worth ending. I was George Bailey on the bridge, the big-dreaming banker who'd fallen on hard times, staring into the emptiness, and there was no Clarence, no guardian angel, no help, no basket of cash, and no happy ending.

Dead or alive, my time was running short. The end of my freedom could come at any moment. I didn't know what I would be charged with or when. But my life was in a constant state of fear. I was always looking over my shoulder, studying my surroundings, wondering if this would be the day. Every minute took me closer to the inevitable.

Drip.

On Thursday, April 14, 2016, I went to Jeff City to meet with our attorney about business and to have drinks with friends.

Afterward, my son Jack had a baseball game. I sat down near home plate on the first base side. We were the visiting team, and Jack was up second, on deck. I was getting ready to watch him hit when I got a tap on the shoulder.

It was an FBI agent.

"Come with me," he said.

I turned the corner and there were six of them, as if I was going to flee.

My attorney had told me I would get called in to self-surrender, post bond, and go home.

The agent walked me away from the baseball game to a nearby

parking lot, turned me around, frisked me, and emptied my pockets. Hands behind my back, he took my wallet and car keys and gave them to my wife. Cold, hard steel clicked around my wrists. *You have the right to remain silent.* My shoulders sank. I was led away in handcuffs. My life would never be the same.

CHAPTER 12
FROM THE BIG TIME
TO THE BIG HOUSE

When you crash and burn, there isn't always a singular rock bottom—at least there wasn't for me.

The day of my arrest was one of my lowest points. I was so ashamed for my family. My actions had put everything at risk. *I'd been arrested at my son's baseball game.* They could have coordinated a time with my lawyer and called me into an office. Instead, they infiltrated the only unblemished part of my life.

After I was arrested, the agents took me to a St. Louis County detention center that housed violent criminals for the night. "Don Trump's here," they announced, because I was a tall White guy who fit the general description of the real estate icon and soon-to-be president.

They took my Gucci loafers, alligator belt, and all of my

clothes. When I tried to retrieve them later, they were deemed "missing." Sure. In their place, I slipped on an orange jumpsuit.

I spent one night there with my cellmate. He was little younger than I was and had a son the same age as Jack. He was serving 25 years for second-degree murder. I took the top bunk.

The next morning, they woke me up at 6 a.m. and took me down to the federal building for my arraignment. I was locked up in one of the eight cages for people awaiting their court appearances.

Then I sat and sat and sat, waiting for what seemed like an eternity.

Other arrestees came and went, blabbing to each other about all sorts of incriminating things. "I threw the drugs in a dumpster." *Don't say that!*

There was a collegial aspect to the holding cells.

"Where are you at?"

"Ste. Genevieve. Where are you at?"

"Troy."

I was *finally* called for my hearing and formally charged with one count of bank fraud and one count of misapplication of bank funds. I didn't say much during the hearing *besides yes, ma'am.* The only thing of note I said was recounting how I was arrested at my son's baseball game. This wasn't the time to clear my name. I needed to stand there, nod, and say yes to find out what would happen next.

Michael Litz, my former real estate and business partner, was also indicted.

I stayed locked up at county jail for a few weeks before being freed on bond. Luckily, given the week in custody I had for the child support issue a year earlier, I understood the system. I understood what it was like behind bars. I had a frame of reference.

My release came with tons of stipulations. I had to surrender my passport and participate in mental health evaluation. I had to provide a third-party risk notification to anyone I conducted business with. I also had to submit to computer monitoring and other non-financial conditions of release.

I had to keep the court informed on all of my business activities.

Or else.

I was desperate, depressed, and scared. I had few options, and I was still addicted to the hustle. The legal fees piled up. Bank fraud isn't easy to defend or even understand, and I wanted to pursue every opportunity I could to bring in some money and make things right for my family before I might have to go away for a while.

I pursued deals and business opportunities with a company

selling hair bows and a skin care company, while the adult daycare business still operated in the background.

"The journey has begun," I wrote in a pitch email, striking an uplifting note.

One scheme involved my company Universal Exports, named after one of James Bond's businesses. I even used a logo pulled from the movie *Quantum of Solace.* I love Bond, James Bond. The court didn't share my affinity, especially since I told my pretrial services officer that the company was defunct when it wasn't.

The government installed tracking software on my computer and collected images from my communications—29,000 of them. The court held a bond revocation hearing where they discussed my business efforts.

"The defendant has repeatedly and willfully obstructed his pretrial supervision as well as repeatedly violated the conditions of his release," my pretrial services officer said, calling me a "financial danger."

This isn't really a thing. But that's the line they used in court, and it got printed in the newspapers. So there I was, the "financial danger" getting shipped off to Warren County Jail in the town of Warrenton. It's known as "a city for all seasons," and I was locked up for all of them. I spent 14 months at Warren County Jail.

I was very familiar with Warrenton. I started doing business there in 1984, and I bought a bank there in 1997.

At Warren County Jail, the male inmates were arranged in three main pods. "A" pod, which included a guy who murdered his family, was relatively quiet. "B" pod was in between. That's where they put me. And then there was "C" pod—a free-for-all. "D" pod was for female inmates, and they would often flash us. Around the corner were the child molesters, who would walk by us to go to the gym. Guys would do everything they could to beat the windows out whenever the child molesters walked past.

There was a code behind bars, a street sense that I needed to sharpen. I always thought my success in banking was due to my street smarts because I had grown up in family business. I knew how things worked on the outside. But these inmates had *street smarts*. I was good at reading people for how they do business. The inmates were reading people for threats and mental health and the angles they could play to get something from you.

Thirty-six men housed in a space made for 24 led to constant conflict and stress. We were left to sleep on the floor on thin little mats. We were typically locked down at 11 p.m. and our cells reopened around 6 a.m. the next morning. Guards would come in and search our belongings once a week, throwing our items everywhere looking for drugs, but really it was just to show us who was in control.

Sometimes the White inmates got their belongings tossed for being White. Sometimes the Black inmates had their items flipped and tossed. I got locked down one time for being White. There was a guy who committed a triple murder and got three life sentences who flooded the building by clogging the toilets with a couple of other inmates. The cells near the flooding held Black inmates, and they felt like there would be a problem if they didn't lock down somebody White. So for three days, I couldn't leave. There was no place to go anyway.

A big source of conflict came with our one shared TV, which was mounted high on the wall and turned to max volume 24 hours a day. The guards handled the remote control. There would be fights at night over which basketball game to watch. But no one cared much about TV in the mornings when I was awake, so I would get the channel changed to country music or halfway intelligent movies.

There were fights over food, too. At mealtime, you had to stand guard over your food and be prepared to move when a fight started. I was a long way from UMB's corporate dining room! There were steel benches, but no one sat on them. We all stood. The guards didn't care if there was a fight and never got in the middle of the little skirmishes.

The food wasn't even worth fighting over. Wednesdays were hot dog days. The hot dogs were weird and misshapen, as if they were cooked in bath water. They tasted like wet socks. A lot of the food tasted that way.

There were times when jail felt like my small-town high school. Everyone knew everything about everybody, and there was a routine and pecking order. There were the bullies and the bullied, the in crowd and the out crowd. For better or worse, we were stuck on this journey together.

Right off the bat, people started pushing me.

"I'll beat the fuck out of you," I snarled. "You want to go at it? Let's go."

I might have been beaten, but I still had fight in me.

Even if I was holding my own and defending myself, I was hurting inside. Depressed. Shamed. Unhealthy. I was carrying my emotions. By the time I entered jail, I had ballooned up to 235 pounds, the heaviest I'd ever been. I was eating horribly unhealthy food night after night, often at Mexican restaurants, stocking up on extra chips and rounds of margaritas.

The tasty food was gone now, and the party was over.

Now the bill had come due, and I was paying for everything.

I had all the time and none of it. Time stood still. Time flew. Time had no purpose. Eventually I would be given a sentence and shipped away to federal prison, and the passage of time would be measurable. But ahead of my sentence, I was just waiting.

And thinking.

I thought about everything that put me here, everything I'd done wrong. Mistakes. Regrets. I'd been living in the gray my entire life, and now I was surrounded by gray bars. My kids hated me, their mothers—forget it. I'd hurt too many people. Bank investors lost money, and the banks failed in part because of my actions. And then there were people scammed by my former business partner Mike Litz who thought they had bought a house and been paying each month, only to find out that he wasn't paying the bank for them after all. Their dreams had turned to dust.

My reputation was mud, and my career was gone.

Yet, somehow, I clung to hope. Hope that I could repair some of the relationships I'd fractured. That I could turn my life around and provide for my family. That I could make things right. That I could forgive myself.

Walking and religion gave me purpose and focus.

The gym wasn't widely used during the mornings, so I typically went early in the day. The guards would buzz the door, I would walk down the hall, and they would buzz me into the gym so I could walk on a treadmill for an hour alone. Getting buzzed through the doors felt like entering a jewelry store. But here, there really wasn't anything valuable to take besides dignity.

I often walked in the pod, too. It was 54 feet down the long hallway, and I would walk back and forth along that hallway. Fifty-four. What a random number. When you have time to think, you think about the most random little things.

Between the gym and the hallway, I walked at least 10 miles a day, which helped me lose the excess weight I'd put on, and then some.

Religion, meanwhile, soothed my soul. Prior to my incarceration, I went to church each Sunday. I did this out of a social obligation, and the lessons and scriptures didn't really connect until I went away. I held Bible study in my cell each night, and sometimes more than a dozen people would show up. The guards can listen to your conversations in your cells, and they began listening in, thinking that something was going on besides Bible study.

It was haunting to learn the depths of some of the inmates' suffering. A young man came in one night, and after several minutes of silence, with everyone gone, I asked him what was wrong. For some reason, I asked him a question I've never asked anyone in my life. There was an energy I felt.

"There's something on your mind, something you're not telling me. Were you sexually abused?"

"My brother sexually abused me," he said, choking back tears. "We concocted a story to blame our grandfather."

The lie, he told me, set off a chain of falling dominoes that destroyed his family. It fueled their parents' divorce. His relationship with his father deteriorated because of his mother's hatred for the grandfather.

He cried and cried. He became a drug addict to soften his pain, and he and his brother had both been addicts and bounced in and out of the criminal justice system. He was about 30 at the time, my son Stephen's age. The whole story broke my heart.

So many of the inmates were damaged by similar factors: drugs, a lack of education, or limited fatherly support in their lives. The patterns were tragic. A disproportionate number of them were Black or Hispanic.

I was surrounded by so many broken people and saw an opportunity to help. I tried to teach the other inmates, talking to them in a fatherly way. I got them to read better books. Do I know if I made any difference? I don't know. I doubt it. But I tried, and that was the beginning of my redemption.

Trust and an unassuming nature helped me build rapport with my fellow inmates. After a while, I was seen as one of the guys, an older, more seasoned White representative of the prisoners and was nicknamed "the podfather." Quite a departure from my *godfather* days when I had banking power and influence. In prison, the name godfather was reserved for Don, an older Black man. He and I teamed up to keep the peace among the men. There was some fighting, of course, but it wasn't out of control. I even earned the right to watch the TV on my channel from 7 a.m. until noon each day. That was a big deal.

One night a few months into my stint in jail, I was hungry. All the walking and lack of calories was starting to have an impact. I was also about as depressed as I've ever been. I paced up and down the hallway looking for something, for a sign.

There was a young inmate we called the "Unabomber." He was always trying to short out the electricity in the pod. He was diabetic and got food every night, and he tossed me an apple when he walked by.

"God, thank you," I told him.

That little gesture of humanity from "Unabomber" told me God was going to get me through this. It felt, all of a sudden, like

I had hope. Hope was the only thing helping me through this. Especially since it took so long for my case to wind through the court.

On court days, I'd get dragged out of bed at 4:30 a.m., taken downstairs, chained, and put in leg irons. I never went to court without being chained and cuffed. It wasn't a typical practice for white-collar, nonviolent criminals. I'm not sure why I was treated differently.

The season changed from spring to summer to the fall—football season.

The inmates who gambled had a football pool going. I would answer people's questions and pick the spread, and usually I'd get 10 or so out of 11 games right, so they would throw me soup or other food, and then I learned how to trade the food I didn't like for the food I did like.

As a result of those efforts, I gained a second nickname— *Google*. I had information, some from my own brain and some from sneaking glances at the guards' phone. The inmates took care of me because I took care of them.

And yet, through most of football season, I was still waiting for my trial to begin. By Thanksgiving, the U.S. Attorney's Office started talking to my attorney about a deal. If I went to trial—a bad idea for federal cases, which have a high conviction rate, especially where the evidence is clear-cut—I could be staring at 20 years.

Now was not the time to fight.

It was time to roll over and take whatever they were going to give me. *Thank you, your honor.* The federal sentencing guidelines based on the crimes I would plead guilty to—bank fraud and misapplication of bank funds—came with the expectation of a 46-month sentence, with a range of 37 to 46 months depending on a range of factors like my behavior. Three or four years.

If I did what I was told, I could be out by July 1, 2020—less than three years away, since the time I'd already spent behind bars would contribute toward my sentence. If this was high school, that would put me most of my way through freshman year.

It's lonely to count the days, months, and years when they all feel the same—drab and emotionless, the same day over and over. And it wasn't like people were lining up to call or visit me.

Jeanette was the one person who served as a beacon during my darkest points.

We talked at least once and often twice a day. We had met before I was arrested, and on December 23, 2017, my attorney brought Jeannette out to surprise me. It was a wonderful moment in a horrible period in my life.

She continued to visit from time to time, using paperwork that identified her as an assistant on my case. Like the apple from the Unabomber, Jeannette's support brought me hope.

Another sign emerged when one of the supervisors pulled me

aside. I was starving, down to 160 pounds, and he got me an extra serving of cereal and milk every morning and a protein shake every night, and my weight stabilized.

People cared about me, even when I struggled to find the value in my own life. I reflected that care back onto others, serving as a de facto advocate for my fellow inmates. There was one point when a young 30-year-old inmate had rubbed some other inmates the wrong way, and they wanted him out—he was liable to get attacked. Things got tense. The guards didn't care. I got up and stood on the steel picnic table. "We're not gonna throw this guy out," I said. I got consensus from some other inmates, and it all got straightened out.

Another time, I got a new cell assignment at the end of a hall that was 60 degrees but, because of its location, pin-drop quiet. Two Hispanic inmates bunked with me—everyone knew I wouldn't let them get taken advantage of because of their broken English.

One day, a large inmate was picking on one of my bunkmates for some reason. I came storming out and started threatening him. You would've thought air-raid sirens were going off. Half a dozen men came flying down the stairs to protect me.

"Shaun, we'll do anything for you, but please don't start a fight this early in the morning," they said.

As 2017 turned to 2018, my guilty plea was locked in. If I didn't plead guilty, I would be finished—the superseding indictment against me included 10 counts. If, hypothetically, I could beat the government on one count, they could turn around and try me on another count.

In May 2018, I was sentenced to 68 months. Five-and-a-half years. That would put my release somewhere around November 2021.

Separately, Mike and Tim Murphy, the primary loan officer at Excel, both pleaded guilty to two counts, too. Mike was sentenced to three years and forced to pay restitution, while Tim got probation.

"I've hurt many people. I can never repair the harm that I've done," I told the court during my sentencing hearing. Many critics believed my sentence was too lenient. They suggested I would continue to rip people off as long as I had "access to a phone and face-to-face opportunities."

But who I was when I committed those crimes wasn't the person I was when I was sentenced. I had learned a painful lesson.

With my sentence secured, I would soon be transferred to federal prison.

At 4:30 a.m. on the first day of summer, 2018, the guards came to my cell. "Put your clothes on. You are being shipped out. You can't take anything with you." Luckily, the only things of value I had were pads and pens. I had stopped writing "results" on them by this point. I slipped the paper and pens to some of the remaining inmates I'd connected with.

They drove us inmates to MidAmerica St. Louis Airport, a big government boondoggle opened 20-some years ago. They stopped our van right before we entered the airport because they wanted to consolidate us on three county deputy trucks, so I got outside for 20 feet. I couldn't believe it. The sunshine felt so warm and inviting. I had missed it so much.

As we stood there, a plane pulled up, and it was circled by security carrying AR-15s. There was enough hardware to start a war. Guards unloaded the prisoners arriving on the plane and loaded up the new ones.

I was transferred to a bus headed for United States Penitentiary, Marion in Marion, Illinois, built in the 1960s to replace the prison on Alcatraz Island in California's San Francisco Bay. John Gotti once served time at Marion—it used to be the nation's toughest federal prison. I rode over with a bunch of guys. They gave us a bologna sandwich, chips, and juice. A guy behind me was all cuffed up but kind of friendly. We started chatting.

Someone else a few rows behind us warned me. "He's a fucking *chomo*. Don't get near him." Everybody on that bus besides that guy and I must have been child molesters.

Ugh.

We got to the Marion main prison, and they let me out in front.

"You're going to camp, stand over here," a man told me. He took my shoes and clothes—my only supplies. So now I'm not only outside on this beautiful sunny day, but I also have nothing on me.

I'm just standing there, wondering what the hell was happening. A driver swerved up in a Dodge minivan and slammed on the breaks.

"Who's going to camp?"

I begrudgingly raised my hand and climbed into the back of his minivan along with about eight others. There were no guards. *Was this official? Was this even happening? What the hell was camp?* This guy drove like a bat out of hell. I thought I was going to die.

We arrived at "camp," Marion's minimum-security satellite facility, and piled out of the van. An Asian man, Art Lee, came up to me. "You must be Shaun Hayes," he told me. *Yep.* "We are glad to have you. Doug Cassity is looking forward to seeing you, and they are having a dinner for you tonight."

Oh. This was different.

Doug was from St. Louis and had done business with UMB and Allegiant and I had met him many years earlier. He got busted in a prearranged funeral scam. I didn't know him well before prison, but he was very good to me behind bars.

At first, I worried about being singled out. And then I recognized it was a good thing. I got processed quickly and received temporary clothes and horrible boat shoes. I visited my bunk and luckily it was in a good spot.

I had a great, refreshing bath in the dormitory-style bathroom. At dinnertime, instead of heading to the chow hall and eating with the other inmates, I got pulled aside.

"We're going to the gym," they said. There, we ate steak fajitas. A big step up from the soggy hot dogs. The next night we had steaks.

I was part of the "white-collar group" now.

In prison, you associate with people from your city—the term is called "cars." I wasn't really part of a car. I was looked at differently. Since I grew up in a small town and ran banks in Black communities, and given my 14 months in county jail, I could talk to just about anybody.

I had knowledge and could help people. That's why people called me the godfather, or rather, the podfather.

CHAPTER 13
CAMP

Federal prison felt like a bad summer camp.

It was a bunch of rough-around-the-edges guys roughing it with passable food and little supervision. At Marion, drugs, alcohol, and food flowed in from the outside, and some of the inmates even made money running items through the woods. There was no fence.

There was contentment among the inmates at Marion. We didn't have to work, and little was asked of us. But we also recognized that if we did anything too egregious, we were liable to go somewhere worse—somewhere more guarded, locked down, and restrictive. There was also a greater potential to have time added to our sentences.

Unlike county jail where the TV was a central focus (and something to fight about), here TV was an afterthought. At Marion, the inmates were more inclined to read books, play dominoes and cards, shoot pool, and exercise.

I didn't have to fight over my food anymore, either. I didn't have to fight about anything.

The prison was full of mostly drug dealers, with some white-collar criminals like me and Doug Cassity mixed in. Doug took me under his wing, and I wound up getting a dorm near him. He showed me the ropes and made me feel comfortable in my new setting.

Mike Litz, the business partner whose financial problems had precipitated the poor decisions that sent me to prison, was set to report to Marion in July 2018, a few weeks after I arrived. He never showed. His body was later found at a motel.

I hadn't been in touch with Mike for years as we endured our legal issues, but my heart hurt for him and his family when I learned of his death. Suicide had crossed my mind many times. I understood far too well the emotional weight Mike had been carrying.

But being sent to jail, and later prison, recentered me. Talking to a therapist also helped. I wanted to make things better, and being dead wouldn't help me do that. Through my time in custody, I started to realize that I still had purpose and that there was hope in tomorrow.

Hope kept me from ending my life, and it carried me through my darkest days. My dad had been dead for years, but I could still hear his voice. *It could always be worse.*

As soon as I got to camp, other inmates told me about RDAP, which stands for Residential Drug Abuse Program (despite the name, participants can be battling numerous issues, not just drug abuse). Completing RDAP could trim a year off my sentence, and I thought that maybe the program would also teach me something about myself.

I asked around and found out I probably qualified for RDAP. Unfortunately, they weren't conducting interviews for the next enrollment period until November or December, which was nearly half a year away.

So, I had to wait.

Time seemed to move faster in prison. It helped having a goal, a destination, and an end date in mind. When I was in county jail, I didn't know what my sentence would be, so waiting there meant waiting for what's next. In prison, I was waiting to go home.

On the day of the interviews for RDAP, my friend Randy went first. He approached me afterward with a grin.

"I got in," he said. "I'm going to Montgomery, Alabama. You're going to get in, too."

He proceeded to recount the questions they asked him so I could prepare. My interview came an hour later. I answered the questions truthfully and honestly. I got in, too, talking about my problem drinking and emotional struggles.

"Where do you want to go?" the interviewer asked me.

"Pensacola," I said. "I heard it was the hardest program, but

I also wanted to go somewhere warm." Illinois in winter didn't appeal to me.

I was approved for Florida. But there was a snag. The United States government was shut down in late December 2018 and into January 2019 over funding, which meant my transfer stalled until late February. When you're in prison, you're at the whim of factors far outside of your control.

But this transfer wasn't like my previous one where I'd been shuttled on a bus with child predators and a cascade of armed guards. Instead, I was loaded up in a car with my box of stuff and dumped in front of a motel to stand in 20-degree weather for two hours waiting for a Greyhound bus. The air chilled my lungs.

The bus pulled up and I walked up the steps as if I was just another traveler. To my delight, there was Jeannette. She was, at this point, the closest person in my life. We had planned this all out. She took the bus from St. Louis so we could ride down together to Nashville. We talked the entire way and had a four-hour layover.

We then rode the bus to Birmingham, and in Montgomery I stopped and had lunch with my son Stephen. In Mobile, I met with my nephew Haymes, who brought me a cheeseburger and fries, and it was just about the best cheeseburger I'd ever had.

Next it was on to Federal Prison Camp, Pensacola, which is located on a naval base. This meant activity in the form of planes and cars and traffic and life. It sure beat looking out at the woods! I visited with the head of psychology the day after I arrived.

"I'm here for RDAP," I said.

"Well, you need to talk to Dr. Profitt. He's in the psychology building. He ought to be there around one o'clock." It was noon. So at about five to one, I entered the psychology building and walked down the hall. I heard someone behind me and turned around to see a tall, thin man coming toward me.

"Excuse me, sir. I'm looking for Dr. Profitt," I said.

"I'm Dr. Profitt."

Thank God. I explained my situation and my approval to enter the program.

"Our next class starts May 18," he told me, which was nearly three months away (it was February 27). That would mean I'd be done in February.

"Well, I'm already approved."

"Come into my office," he told me. His office was covered with University of Kentucky basketball and St. Louis Blues gear. I almost owned that team once, and now I was looking at the logo as a prison inmate. He hopped on his computer and made a call, and next thing I knew, I was going to "D" dorm to commence my RDAP program. Everyone in the program stayed in the same dorm.

The current class started one week earlier, and if I had shown up the following day, I wouldn't have been able to join. As a result of that encounter, I got into the February program instead of having to wait until May, which turned out to be a miracle.

The RDAP program ran like the military. Everything had to be precise—our uniforms, our bunks, our living space, and our behavior. The class started with 37 people. Before we were done, more than half had dropped out.

Many people snapped from the pressure.

Pensacola was known for being a cushy prison assignment but had an especially difficult RDAP program. Dr. Profitt was a big reason why. He was *tough*, and that toughness was exactly what I needed.

We were held to a high standard. No drinking, no smoking, no gambling. If we stumbled or messed up, it could cost us a full year, as we would have to restart the program.

I felt like I'd joined a cult. They have certain sayings—recitals meant to make you think about yourself and your day and reinforce the process you were going through. You can't speak until you're spoken to. Everything has a system. And I'm thinking, *fuck, what did I get myself into?*

The meetings started exactly at 7:30 a.m. and ended exactly at nine. We addressed each other formally.

They drew names out of a box, and if your name was pulled, you had to get up and explain your mistakes or struggles, focusing on a dozen different topic areas. When the class started, I was terrified by the prospect of having my name called. I wanted to do the bare minimum, skate by, get my 12 months in, and go on with my life.

The first time I got up, I looked like a total idiot. Though I'd been there a couple of weeks, I stammered and stumbled, struggling to share my feelings.

Mr. Hayes kept getting called. I paid attention to the patterns and processes of the sessions. Over time, I got really good at opening up to the group. I shared the ten things I had screwed up instead of just one or two and often volunteered to discuss a key thought of the day. The more information I provided and the more wrongs I shared, the more progress I made.

"Today, my thought of the day is gratitude. And I believe that gratitude has changed my life, because I understand now that I wasn't grateful for my family and for the relationships I've had in my life. Now I not only have gratitude for that, but I also have gratitude that I'm not drinking alcohol," I'd tell the group.

We went from those meetings to classes, where we rotated between three different psychologists over three different programs with beginning, intermediate, and end stages. I actually won one of the three awards at the end of the program.

I kept advancing with the help of some lucky breaks. I got introduced to the guy who assigned jobs. My job was to clean the bus shed on Saturday and Sunday nights. The catch? There were no buses in the shed on those nights. They paid me a whopping eight dollars a month to do nothing. After I'd been there eight or nine months, the RDAP personnel steered me toward clerical work. "Gosh, you have all these skills, we want you to come work with us," they said. I ended up working as a secretary in the psychology department, setting schedules, making copies, and doing other menial tasks.

The program was everything I needed it to be. But near the end of the program, I started to feel physically *horrible*. Something wasn't right.

Still, I didn't complain. If I told anyone I might have a health issue, I'd have to start the program over again, and I was *so close* to finishing.

This program was about more than just getting a reduced sentence—I was finally looking inward and focusing on rational thinking. Through this program, I learned that I don't control anything. My lack of control wasn't an excuse to do whatever I wanted. Instead, it provided me with an inner peace to be able to deal with anything that popped up. So much of my life was based on control, and I wasn't trying to control situations anymore.

I powered through despite my poor health and graduated from the program. Soon enough, I was headed back to Marion. I wanted to serve out the remainder of my sentence at "camp."

Jeannette drove down and picked me up. We had breakfast with my nephew and lunch with my son. We went to a white tablecloth restaurant in Nashville for dinner, and I ate tuna. I called Marion from Nashville.

"Traffic's really bad. I'm going to be late," I said. They didn't care. I arrived at 9:30 p.m. instead of 8 o'clock, and I spent the night in the hole of the big prison because it was too late at night for intake. There was no heat, and I only got sicker, damn near freezing to death. The next day I was back at camp.

One female guard—everyone there loved her—checked up on me.

"You're so sick," she said with worry in her voice.

She got them to take me to the hospital, where I watched classic movies on TV and ate whatever I wanted. They took such good care of me.

I bounced back and forth between the hospital and doctor's visits, and still, no one could find what was wrong. The doctor had me come back for another checkup in early April. I worried that continued medical interventions would require me to stay in prison longer.

"If you tell them the truth that I need to come back, they won't let me out on time," I told him.

"You promise you'll go to doctor when you get out?" the doc asked.

"Yes," I said.

In order to get out, I needed to spend the 15 days before my release in solitary confinement since the COVID-19 pandemic was raging. I had 15 minutes outside of my cell each day to take a shower and make a phone call.

I slept on concrete using only the thin little mat they provided. I couldn't go anywhere, and my body felt like a rusted chain.

They put my meals through a little hole in the door. If I stood at the door I could watch TV, but I couldn't change the channel.

Fifteen long, empty days.

I got out on May 5, 2020, after 37 months behind bars. I was sent to live in a halfway house, but due to the pandemic, I was fitted with an ankle monitor and sent away, living instead in a nearby apartment.

I was out. Free.

But I still had lots of repair work ahead, and I still didn't know what was wrong with me.

CHAPTER 14
OUTSIDE

Back on the outside, I trudged along.

My mysterious health issues lingered like a mysterious shadow. Was it a heart problem? A lung problem? None of it made a lot of sense. I went for some tests, but they were inconclusive. I tried to brush it all aside.

I wanted to move forward, which wasn't so easy. After spending three years on the inside, I had grown accustomed to the structure of having decisions made for me. Not much thought was needed on a day-by-day basis. Inside, I couldn't go anywhere. I was awake at a certain time, fed at a certain time, and in bed at a certain time.

Behind bars, people didn't bother me. I was secure.

In a world of criminals, I was seen as a resource.

In the outside world, I was seen as a criminal. A fraudster. A letdown. I had gone from shaking everyone's hand years earlier to now shying away from people—in part because I didn't know how they would respond to seeing me.

Some people went out of their way to avoid me, and that was okay.

Others grew agitated and bitter. I deserved that too.

I appreciated those who stood by me, including Jeannette, who had been so supportive of me during my time in prison. She tried to help me get back on my feet.

Unfortunately, the relationship didn't last. She was there when I needed someone the most and she made the days livable. I'll be forever grateful for that.

On the outside, I had to figure out how to make a living again. There was so much I couldn't do—my list of restrictions and stipulations was as long as a river, and my probation was scheduled to last for five years.

Banking was out, obviously, but I also couldn't be self-employed or employed as a consultant. Opening additional lines of credit or incurring new credit charges without permission weren't allowed either.

They wanted me to get a standard 30-hours-a-week job "at a lawful type of employment." So loan sharking was out, I guessed.

I tried to find a path forward through other business opportunities. Call it pride, ego, or faith, but I didn't see the problems at the time.

Learning isn't always linear, and I was still learning to live inside the boundaries and color within the lines.

As I reestablished myself, I tried to repair my relationships with my children. It's been easier with some of them than others based on their ages and stages in life. I'd let them down, disrupted their lives, embarrassed them, and simply wasn't there. I feel horrible about that, and I'm so sorry.

So, so sorry.

I think daily of the pain I've caused—both to those I love and to those I don't know. Will that ever fully go away? I don't know. It hasn't gone away for me so far. At the end of the day, I know in my heart that I didn't do anything intentionally or maliciously to hurt anyone.

That, however, doesn't erase the fact that my decisions hurt people. And I continue to carry that burden.

Like I said, I trudged along. On Easter Sunday, 2021, instead of celebrating with my family or friends, I was at the hospital. All my energy had drained from my body. I felt *horrible* and was barely able to walk. The doctors and nurses poked and prodded to see what was wrong.

Hemoglobin is the protein in red blood cells that carries oxygen. A normal hemoglobin count is between 13 and 17, and mine registered at 5.

The mystery illness, as it turned out, was cancer. It was back again, and I was diagnosed with non-Hodgkin's lymphoma. The doctors put me on blood transfusions and chemotherapy. They put new blood into my body in one procedure and filled my body with toxic chemicals in the next. At one point, they gave me a transfusion of cold blood. I had an extreme reaction and wound up back at the hospital.

I thought I was going to die.

I continued with chemotherapy for four or five months. The chemo didn't make me sick, thankfully, but I remained weak since my blood count was still dangerously low. One time, I fainted at my son's football game and had to be rushed to the hospital.

After months of treatment, I found myself in remission. I was feeling pretty good again. I had survived prison and a battle with cancer.

I also needed hernia surgery, and as I recovered, I developed an infection in my right middle finger. It wasn't healing. Antibiotics didn't seem to be working, and while I was dealing with this finger infection, I started coughing.

A deep, dry, persistent cough.

I struggled to breathe. My lungs were on fire. By January 2022, I went to the ER and didn't get out of bed until March 2.

It was pneumonia. A pulmonologist and internist both confirmed it. One form was bacterial. The other was "Covid pneumonia," as they called it, which is a lingering byproduct of the virus that was circling the globe.

I still have shortness of breath, congestion, and lots of phlegm to this day.

Getting sick slowed me down and refocused me. When you think you're going to die, you take stock of your life and what you wish to do with your remaining time.

It also made me realize that I wanted to use my time to help others. I can't undo the damage I caused. I can only try to balance the sheet. The younger generation talks about "paying it forward," and now it's my time to do the same.

Paying it forward is an easier process than paying it back. I still owe five million dollars in restitution. A chunk of my income gets taken away each month.

I started thinking about giving speeches and writing a book to share my story in hopes that it can help others. I believe I have something of value to impart. If I had been *only* a success or *only* a failure, what would I really have to say? Attaining true, tangible success only to see it come crashing down gives me a level of insight I wouldn't otherwise have.

For the short-term, being bed-bound made it difficult for me to fulfill the conditions of my probation. The court wanted me to secure that 30-hour-week job. But I was sick and dragging.

The government became interested in my business efforts

from the previous year, too. Investigators obtained phone and email records showing my business connections and personal dealings. Nothing I did was criminal—but it was the type of activity restricted under the terms of my release and was something I should've been more mindful of.

My health was just starting to turn the corner, and here I was, facing another fight for my freedom.

At my court hearing, they didn't even need to prove that I had violated the terms of my probation. Only the whisper or accusation of a violation was enough to send me back to jail for 30 days.

The government wanted no gray, and I needed a reminder of what that meant.

My hearing was originally scheduled for April but was pushed back until May. I met with my lawyer and tried to mount a defense, but there wasn't much I could do.

My day in court came on May 26.

I pleaded guilty.

I turned myself in the following Tuesday, at which point I would learn my jail assignment. I was back in the system, on the inside again for one month.

Would I go to Kentucky? Florida? Illinois?

I wound up in Ste. Genevieve County Jail in Missouri, about

60 miles south of St. Louis, along the banks of the Missouri River. The bank I'd traded with Jim Dierberg years earlier was in Ste. Genevieve. Just like with Warrenton, I was back in jail where I once had a bank.

Recidivism is common among federal prison inmates—roughly half are bound to get re-arrested in the next eight years.[3] The stigma follows you and makes the transition to the outside pretty brutal. Good luck applying to jobs! I've been turned down for a job making hospital beds. Everyone was thrilled about me working there until I had to check the box that I was a convicted felon, and then that was that. Somehow, my bank fraud conviction was a deal-breaker for me working second shift changing sheets.

I was even turned down for a job at the morgue. One moment they were "so excited" to have me join the team. The next, they were leaving me a cold, emotionless voicemail message. "Due to the findings on your background check, we will not be able to continue your onboarding process."

As a country, we spend so much time and effort and energy incarcerating people, but not enough time repairing them during and following incarceration. In-custody programs and resources are overall inadequate, and the game is typically stacked against you when you're released—doubly so for minorities and those from lower income classes.

Even with the chips stacked against me, ahead of my reporting

---

3   "Recidivism Among Federal Offenders: A Comprehensive Overview," United States Sentencing Commission, March 2016. https://www.ussc.gov/research/research-reports/recidivism-among-federal-offenders-comprehensive-overview.

back to jail for a month, I felt something I didn't think I would: redemption. Some might look at a return to custody as a setback, but I saw it as an opportunity to refocus, learn, and grow.

I spoke to my nephew on the phone, and he was frantic about me going to jail and getting sick.

"It's okay, it's okay," I reassured him. "I'm not done yet."

When I began my journey in banking, all I wanted to be was a millionaire, and I became that 10 times over. But after I accomplished that goal, I really didn't have another plan. After all of my ups and downs, I finally have my plan—to help influence or improve someone else's life. I want to do something that outlives me.

I want to give back and help others.

I used to own a building in this great spot called Hi-Pointe in St. Louis that was about six or seven miles due west from the Arch. The Hayes Building was named after Alfred Hayes (no relation that I'm aware of), whose company inhabited the building. I met his son probably 20 years ago. I ended up owning that building with my partner. I felt a special connection to it given that my last name was on the building.

When I went to jail for the first time, the building was sold and leveled, and now there's a different building in its place. But that building stood there for a long time. Something that was substantive and important can be destroyed in a moment. And yet, something else can rise in its place—something bigger and grander and new.

It doesn't look like I'll be building new buildings any time soon. But if I can leave a lasting impact and change one person's path, if I can help steer them away from the mistakes I made, I'll die a happy man.

CONCLUSION

I dictate the message into my phone and press send. "I'm five minutes away."

I pull up and park my pickup, grab the bag of hot Chick-fil-A, ring the doorbell, and deliver the meal.

At one point, I was overseeing a $2.5-billion bank. Now I'm zigzagging across suburban St. Louis as a DoorDash delivery driver, handing off meals in the same neighborhoods where I used to approve home loans. Occasionally, I'll be tasked with shopping for groceries or candy for a customer. Or picking up diapers for a mother home alone with her kid.

The work is a stopgap for me, a short-term means of making some additional money. *It's all about cashflow,* right?

I've also been picking up shifts as a school bus driver, shuttling students to and from their homes. Driving a bus provides steadier hours and pay, which the government likes.

For DoorDash, I pop into service for an hour or two at a time and choose delivery zones that aren't far away from my house. A map in the driver app shows me the busiest areas and availability for later in the day if I want to pick up additional work.

Sometimes the recipient doesn't want to meet me, so I take a picture to show where I left the food. Often my deliveries take me past shooting scenes. The police lights and twisted, crumpled dreams are reminders of the things I've lost, the things in my rearview. I keep driving.

After the food is delivered, I receive a rating and my payout, maybe $3 or $4, maybe $10 if someone is feeling really generous, and then it's on to the next delivery.

The ratings fuel me—I still want to win. And even after everything that has happened to me, my customer service skills haven't diminished. Across my early deliveries, my customer rating was 100%. My completion rate was 100%. I was on time or early 92% of the time. I was proud to share my ratings with my friends.

In my past life, I would have looked down at someone delivering food and wondered what went wrong in their life. I don't feel that way now.

I don't care what anybody else thinks. I feel comfortable in my own skin again, and that's such a special thing. People spend their whole lives trying to find themselves, and I can truly say I've found myself.

I don't need to wear a suit, drive a Mercedes, live in a big house, or go into an office every day to feel empowered.

My life isn't perfect, and I still have relationships I need to repair. But I do want to make things right as much as I possibly can. Fortunately, for the first time in probably 15 years, I can see daylight filtering through my windshield once again.

ACKNOWLEDGMENTS

I want to thank God and apologize that it took so long for me to truly trust him. I want to thank my five children whom I love with all my heart. I want to also apologize to them for the pain I have caused them the last several years of my journey. To Kelly, the love of my life, again thank you for everything and I apologize for all the pain I caused you. Haymes, you have helped me in every way the last six years, and for that I am forever grateful.

To Julie, Dan, Elissa, Nicole, Sarah, Shane, and the whole Book Launchers Team, for without whom this book would have only been a dream, thank you.

To the countless coaches, teachers, partners, managers, associates, and friends who have helped me over the years, and also to the many who have helped me in the last seven years of my life, thank you.

Lastly, I want to truly thank all those people who have done horrible things to me because they have made me a better person because of their actions. I am either the most blessed or the luckiest man alive.

LET'S KEEP THE
CONVERSATION
——GOING!——

 Visit shaunhayes.com for more advice on how to successfully navigate your own business journey

 Order special bulk purchases for your company, organization, or community by contacting Jane Fordyce at **jane@shaunhayes.com**

 Book Shaun Hayes for speaking and consultations via **shaunhayes.com/speaking** or **shaun@shaunhayes.com**

 Join Shaun's email list to receive exclusive content and links to Shaun's latest videos. Visit **shaunhayes.com** to sign up.

GET MORE NEWS AND UPDATES

Website: **shaunhayes.com**
Facebook: **Shaun Hayes**
LinkedIn: **Shaun Hayes**
Twitter: **@Shaun74522802**
Instagram: **@shaun_hayes59**
Youtube: **@shaunhayes5037**

THANK YOU
FOR READING!

If you enjoyed **THE GRAY CHOICE**, please leave a review
on Goodreads or on the retailer site where you purchased this book.